Moving & Being Productive in The Midst of Loss
Carol J. Williams

All rights reserved. No part of this publication may be reproduced, stored in a retrieval system, or transmitted in any way, by any means – electronic, mechanical, digital, photocopy, recording, or otherwise – without written permission of the author, except as provided by the United States of America copyright law.

Information noted in this body of work is strictly related to the author's life experiences to the best of her recollection.

Copyright © 2021 by Carol J. Williams

Published by Pecan Tree Publishing, September 2021
Hollywood, FL
www.pecantreebooks.com

Unless otherwise noted, all Scripture quotations are from the King James Version of the Bible from the YouVersion Bible App. Scripture quotations from The Authorized (King James) Version. Rights in the Authorized Version in the United Kingdom are vested in the Crown. Reproduced by permission of the Crown's patentee, Cambridge University Press.

978-1-7372621-3-8 Paperback
978-1-7372621-4-5 Ebook
Library of Congress Control Number: 2021917822

Cover Design by Shaun Johnson/ Shaun Graphics Design
Interior Design by Charlyn Samson

Author Cover Photo Credits:
Make up- Valerie Hawkins
Hair Stylist- Bobby Dunmore
Photographer- DeShone Gales
Wardrobe- Alfreda Copeland

Pecan Tree Publishing
www.pecantreebooks.com

New Voices | New Styles | New Vision –
Creating a New Legacy of Dynamic Authors and Titles
Hollywood, FL

Moving & Being Productive in the Midst of Loss

Carol J. Williams

Preface

No one likes pain. No one wants to lose more than they gain. I can't imagine how Job, whose story is recounted in the Bible, felt. Job lost everything, including his children, in a domino effect within hours. Even with all that Job lost, he kept his posture and belief in God. Yes, though God slew Job, he still trusted The Savior.

Job experienced immense grief! He also had friends who didn't know what to say during his loss! Yet, Job knew somehow that he could not grieve without - God!

Job's ability to keep his posture amid multiple severe losses in one day allowed him to receive double restoration of everything.

No, you don't like the pain associated with the losses you've experienced. No, you don't know how you're going to make it without your loved one. Yes, you're tired of crying. Yes, you're tired of being alone. Yes, you have questions for God. Yes, you feel like God has forsaken and abandoned you.

Well, God has not forsaken or abandoned you! God is with you and for you, even while you're angry with Him in your grief! He still loves you and hasn't changed His mind or promises concerning you.

How do I know this concerning God? I've suffered multiple losses, and not just related to death. I felt abandoned by God and others. I experienced that doubt and insecurity that overwhelms you when you think about living without loved ones. I didn't want to live without them. After years of being stuck in grief without God, God reminded me of who He has always been. Those powerful reminders allowed me to use my pain to move and become productive in the midst of loss.

As I am moving and being productive, I still have moments of intense pain when tears stream down my face. They were present while I was writing this book. I know this book has a purpose; I allowed myself to feel the pain by leaning into it and realizing the purpose of these words is not about me. The purpose of the book is to bring God glory in the Earth. The other purpose is to show individuals a living example that productive and effectual movement can happen as you become productive in the loss.

Are you ready to take the journey to become a person moving and being productive in the midst of loss? Well, let's begin.

Contents

Preface v

Chapter 1: Pain 1

Chapter 2: Losses 18

Chapter 3: Purpose of My Loss 53

Chapter 4: Perspective in the Midst of Loss 68

Chapter 5: Who is God in the Midst of Loss? 74

Chapter 6: Speaking in the Midst of Loss 78

Chapter 7: Promises in the Midst of Loss 84

Chapter 8: Prayers in the Midst of Loss 87

Chapter 1

Pain

Whether we want to admit it or not, pain is part of the grief process. I don't know anyone who likes pain. I most certainly don't like it. Pain is a part of our growth process. If you're like me, you wish the Lord would choose another way to help growth.

When I think of pain, I appreciate Jesus' love for us even more. If I had a choice to come off The Cross, I would've been like, "See you all later! I am coming down from this Cross." Jesus didn't do that. The amazing part is Jesus took the pain without numbing the pain.

The medical world views pain as being subjective and objective. When pain is subjective, it's what the patient is telling medical personnel. When the pain is objective, it's what medical personnel sees. The assessment of pain is completed by asking a patient to rate the pain on a scale of 1-10, with ten being the worst. Patients are asked the location, the intensity, the frequency, and the duration of pain. The purpose of asking these questions is to understand how to treat the pain.

Pain is treated adequately if patients are truthful concerning its presence. I remember working as a Registered Nurse on a medical-surgical unit, assessing patients' pain. I did experience patients telling me their pain was a two (subjective), but objective (facial grimaces) manifested a higher rate. The score of two didn't require any intervention. Here's a question for you: do you feel the patient endured unnecessary pain related to not telling the truth? Are we enduring unnecessary pain because we're not truthful to others? Our untruth is manifested when someone asks us how we are doing, and our response is fine. Often, we're not fine; we're hurting. It's okay to articulate I AM HURTING.

The pain I've experienced over the years has been real. I can't tell you how many nights I cried and asked God why so much pain. After all these years of pain, I discovered God is present in my silent tears and silent frustrations. I thought the pain I experienced was only related to the loss of loved ones. I discovered; however, the pain was also related to other losses in my world.

My mother told me I was a miracle child. She gave birth to my sister on her birthday. Then, after multiple miscarriages and being told she would not have more children, she gave birth to me. Sleeping one night, she had a vision of her deceased mother carrying a baby across a body of water. My mother believed the dream meant she was pregnant; and promised if she were, she would give the child back to the Lord and raise the child in church. She was, unknowingly, already three months pregnant when she had that dream. She discovered this after going to the doctor because she was not feeling well. I always wondered how a miracle child could have a life full of pain starting from an early age!

All my life, I had to fight to be. I believe this is part of my struggle with being all God has called me to be. While I am writing, I discovered my first loss is a relationship. I always wanted a relationship with my mother like I saw others have with their mothers. I longed to tell my mother that family members were molesting me. However, I was afraid she wouldn't believe me, or worse, she would chastise me.

Growing up, all I heard about was God and how to live and be holy. My mother always told me sex before marriage was a sin. I struggled with telling her about the molestation believing I had committed a sin. I struggled with telling her because she believed I was a virgin. I lived to try to please her; I felt finding out I was not – even though my virginity was lost unwillingly - would add friction to our relationship. I dealt with the molestation and not being able to tell the one person I should have been able to confide in by becoming rebellious and resentful toward my mother. Still, I wanted my mother to understand I needed her and not things.

Although I didn't know how to handle being molested as a young person, years later, I felt one correct way to handle it was by confronting those who molested me, even if they didn't believe me. I held the secret for years. I remember reading Author/Televangelist Joyce Myers' book, *Beauty for Ashes*; soon after completing the book, I heard Bishop Noel Jones's message, "You're a Gift to Somebody." I sensed the Lord leading me to write a letter to each family member who molested me, expressing the impact of what they had done. Unfortunately, each of them received their letters at the worst time. One received the letter the day of their father's death. The other family member received the letter the day of their father's funeral.

I thought I made the wrong decision, but I knew the Lord instructed me to write the letters and send them. I was instructed to do this because I would be speaking in front of one of them one day, and I needed to make sure I was free from the pain enough to speak without a flashback or emotional response. That came to pass when I was asked to do the eulogy for a family member. As I was speaking, I happened to look up and notice one of the abusers sitting on the front row directly in front of me. I silently whispered a prayer asking the Lord's help to stay focused on the assignment. I was grateful to the Lord for the ability not to be triggered by their presence.

The letters written to everyone described the effects of the molestation. I was expecting an apology. The first and second person apologized and mentioned not knowing the impact of the molestation. We became closer because I wrote the letter, forgave them, and accepted their forgiveness. I forgave the other person, though they never acknowledged anything happened until revisiting the incident. I am a Co-Author for *Beyond the Pretty Dress* by E-Claudette Freeman. My story talked about being molested by family members. I never mentioned anyone's name. I thought it would be right to inform the individual of the molestation before the book was released. They didn't speak to me for months. When we would see each other, I felt the tension, not knowing why. I discovered it was because I mentioned the molestation in the book. When we did speak, I was surprised when they asked, "Who were you molested by?" It was like they had amnesia. Yes, there was penetration, but it was the mention of them placing their penis in my mouth and peeing in my mouth that triggered their memory. They then apologized. I accepted their apology and let them know I had forgiven them when I wrote the letter they never acknowledged.

In life, we have certain expectations from our family members they cannot fulfill for whatever reason. Often, other family members fulfill our expectations, and we don't recognize them or appreciate them.

The molestation caused a loss of relationship with my mother and a loss of relationship with the two abusers' parents. I spent years being jealous of them and their relationship with their children. It appeared they had the perfect relationship. Their children could have a conversation with them concerning anything. Here I am, the child whose mom only talked to her about God and never life and its experiences.

The jealously turned into anger and resentment. I felt I was paying the price at the hands of their children, so the least they could do was work on building a relationship with me. I wasted years of energy trying to develop a relationship out of unhealthy emotions and vindication. I can't expect anyone to give me anything they can't provide or want to share.

The Lord gave me the strength in January 2021 to finally have the conversation with the parents and disclose that two of their children had molested me. I told them about feeling they owed me. I shared how I believed they were responsible for establishing a relationship with me since I endured pain at their children's hands. I told them how I always wanted to have a relationship with them but couldn't because of the massive elephant in the room. They were astonished to hear my truth, apologized for what happened, and told me they hated what I had gone through. I explained I held the information secretly for years, but I wanted them to know because I knew I would be sharing it in the written form again.

Transparently, they shared that it wasn't fair to hold them hostage to something they knew nothing about. They offered this apology, "Carol, I hate this happened to you. I wish you would have told me after the incident." I immediately felt a lifting from my heart. Some things we think are about us are not. I learned from the conversation that although I wanted and expected them to have a relationship with me, they could not supply what I needed. It was nothing against me; my expectations weren't realistic.

The lesson I learned that day and looking at things in hindsight is evaluating and shifting my expectations may be necessary. It's imperative to assess our expectations of others during loss. What are we expecting from individuals? Are our expectations realistic? Are we able to meet the expectations we're asking others to meet? Are the expectations able to be met by the individuals? Once we ask these challenging questions, our expectations will shift. We will discover individuals may not be able to meet our expectations. However, the Lord can and will meet our expectations according to His will and purpose for our lives. It's essential to allow the Lord to be our expectation. *"My soul, wait thou only upon God; for my expectation is from Him."* (Psalm 62:5 KJV).

I was a child with a challenging relationship with my mother and my peers. During my school years, my peers would make fun of my complexion and size. They would say things like, "it's your world, big girl. It's your class, large a..." I couldn't fight, but I sure could curse someone out! I could cut you well with the trash I talked.

My peers never knew I would go home and cry. I only wanted to be accepted - somewhere. Ironically, out of all things my mother taught me concerning God, not one time did I ever hear that I was accepted by The beloved. I never heard how abundantly He loves me. I never heard that I was a friend of God.

I became tired of life! Life became too much to bear. I decided I wanted to end my life. On one occasion, I went into the bathroom and grabbed a bottle of Tylenol pain relievers. As I stood there, staring at the bottle, thinking about whether I would really do it, I heard a knock on the door. It was my mother. She yelled, "Carol, I know you're in there trying to kill yourself. If you want to kill yourself, don't do it in my house. Go outside and let a bus hit you." Who says this to their child? I am not sure why, but I didn't go through taking the Tylenol or going outside as my mother instructed to let a bus hit me.

During my school years, I experienced the kind of friendship I wanted when I met Barbara Lawrence. She loved me for me. We were not only connected in the natural but the spirit as well. We both were full-figured, dark-skinned girls who loved to eat, shop, and sing. We were connected spiritually by knowing when something was going on with one another. It was not unusual for one of us to reach out to the other to pray. My thoughts of suicide continued. The next time the suicidal thoughts overwhelmed me came during a flashback of my mother believing a pastor who spoke negative words concerning me to her. I went to my room with the pills in my hand and closed the door. My phone rang several times. I ignored it initially, but the persistent ringing annoyed me, so I finally answered it. It was Barbara. Before I could say anything, she spoke, "Carol, the Lord told me to call you and ask what's in your hand? Carol, what's in your hand?" I was holding the phone while looking at the pills in my hand. I took a long sigh and answered, "I have pills in my hand." The tears started streaming down my face. I told her, "Barbara, I can't take this anymore. I am tired of living."

I appreciate Barbara! She didn't know what to say at that moment. The next voice I heard was her mother, Doreen. Barbara clearly couldn't handle my words. Mrs. Doreen said, "Carol, clearly there's nothing that bad worth killing yourself. Do you need me to come and get you? I will leave my house and come and get you now." Tears were streaming down my face; I said, "No. I will be okay." The truth of the matter is I had no idea if I would be okay.

Prayer had always been a part of my life. I decided before going to sleep to give it a try. "Dear Lord, I really want more out of life. If you would just let me sleep, I will go to church in the morning. I ask you, Lord, please speak to me through Your Word tomorrow. In Jesus', Name I pray, Amen!

I believe the Lord has a sense of humor. He did allow me to sleep and get up! However, He didn't speak to me through The Word. I left the church more wounded. I am not even sure what the title of the pastor's message was. The only part of it that stood out was, "I don't know why anyone would want to kill themselves. I love myself! Something must be wrong with you if you want to kill yourself." I couldn't believe what I was hearing. Once I reached my car, I sat there and cried. I had no idea what to do! I still felt suicidal.

Suicidal thoughts are real! Please, if you're having thoughts of suicide, reach out for help. It's okay to get help. It takes nothing away from your relationship with God. I didn't know at the time how to reach out for help. I was always told if you kill yourself, you're going to hell. I already felt like I was living in hell on Earth.

I experienced a loss of a friend in seventh grade to suicide. My friend's mother found him hanging in his room. The word on the streets was his parents were upset with him for bringing home a bad grade on his report card since he was always an A student. The pressure to perform for his parents was too much. I recall vividly how he looked in the casket at his funeral. His head seemed more prominent than I had ever seen.

I mentioned earlier that pain is subjective and objective. Loss produces unbearable pain. Subjectively, I presented my pain the time to my friends by saying, "I'm fine." Objectively, my friends were able to see my words were not lining up with my actions. They listened and spoke words of comfort and encouragement.

When you're in pain, it's a blessing to have individuals who can see the pain and speak to it. What do I mean to speak to the pain? I mean having those who can speak The Word of God as a healing balm to the pain. My friends spoke, "Carol, you're going to live and not die to declare the works of the Lord in the land of the living." They spoke, "No weapon formed against you shall prosper." They spoke to the pain!

My friends not only spoke to the pain, but they also prayed I would have the strength to make it through the pain. Lastly, my friends were direct with me concerning needing professional help. During loss, we all need someone who is not going to attend our pity party, even after years of pain. I wanted people to attend my pity celebration. I sent out invitations through visible emotions, conversations, and body language. When you saw me, you saw grief! Grief was my identity. Well, my friends were not coming to the party; and they were direct about declining my invitation.

When my mother died in 2006, I visited her grave regularly. It was convenient because the cemetery was less than 10 minutes away from my house at the time. I remember visiting late in the evening, and as I was leaving, I noticed I had a flat tire. Gratefully, I was able to get help putting the spare tire on the car. For me, that was a sign of moving beyond that morning ritual. I remember thinking about it and asking my mother's spirit, "Mom, you're trying to tell me to stay out of that cemetery, aren't you?"

My friend Teraleen Campbell to this very day, refuses to come to any pity parties of mine. Teraleen is a consistent friend who is direct and tells you the truth even if you don't want to hear it. I went to hear her speak once and we went to dinner afterwards. I am not sure how we got on the conversation of my mother and me going to the cemetery daily. But she asked me, "Carol, how does going to the grave make you feel?" I responded, "I feel sad and depressed?" Teraleen being Teraleen asked, "Then why do you keep going? It doesn't make sense." Admittedly, I was upset. The truth hurts. I had to ask myself, though why did I continue to go.

Why was I going to the cemetery? Why was it hard for me to stop going regardless of the emotional state it left me? Although I know she's not there, going to the cemetery brought the realization of her death. There were times where I wanted to tell her certain things. I will honestly say it never gave me comfort. I had to come to a place in my mind of being okay with not going to the cemetery. Once I told myself that I was okay not to go and not feel bad about going, I was emotionally better. Please be okay with not doing anything that is not emotionally healthy for you during your losses.

When another dear friend had enough of me talking about my mother's death and my emotions, he commanded, "Carol, you need professional help." How dare he tell me that! However, H was right, so I scheduled an appointment with a Christian counselor.

I entered the counselor's office as cool as I could be. Counseling can be painful but helps! As a medical professional, I know that counselors must call for immediate professional assessment or an emergency room visit if they feel a client is a danger to themself. With that knowledge, I had conditioned myself to answer specific questions in a particular manner.

"Carol, are you having thoughts of suicide?" she asked, looking me in the face. I lied. Well, I tried to lie. "No, I am not having thoughts of suicide," I replied. "Okay," she said sharply. "I am going to ask you this one more time, and if you don't tell me the truth, I am picking up this phone…" I wasn't going to be admitted to a psychiatric unit, so angrily, I acknowledged. "Yes, I am having thoughts of suicide."

Genuine friendship/support is revealed in demanding situations. The truth was hard to admit to the counselor, even though she already knew. Her following words will always resonate with me. "Carol, I don't think hell would keep you from killing yourself." I am not sure what the look on my face said, but in my mind, I was wondering if she heard right, "hell won't keep me from killing myself." She advised, "We have to create a safety plan. Who knows you're here?" When I told her, she asked if she could call them. That's exactly what she did, and they created my safety plan. It was their safety plan or a psychiatric unit. I agreed to the plan, which included daily contact and regular follow-ups with the counselor to note any concerns. I had to see the counselor once a week. It's a blessing when your support is consistent with their commitment. My friend followed the instructions given by the counselor. He didn't miss a beat. He got on my nerves. However, I was grateful.

I know it seems like you don't have support through this painful process. You do have support! I want you to be honest with yourself. When has someone seen that you're in pain? What's your response? Is your response to deny it? Is your reply, I am, okay? If that's what you're doing, how can you be upset and feel like no one is there? Let's not push our support away.

Your support may not come from your usual support system! We often look for the same people to be present and miss the opportunity of support when it comes from a different circle of individuals. I expected family and certain friends to be present. However, it didn't happen that way. I had to ask the Lord to help me not become stuck in a place of anger and bitterness with people I expected to be present.

The pain of any loss is real. As I am writing this passage, it's Holy Week! I wonder what was going through Mary's mind as she was watching her son be crucified. It's interesting to note; we don't see or hear about Mary's grief process. Well, Mary was blessed only to have a few days to grieve because her son rose from the grave.

When I think of pain, I think of Jesus and the amount of pain He bore for our freedom from sin. Jesus loved us so much that He endured a painful death. They put a crown of thorns on His head, spat on Him, whipped Him, placed nails in His hands and feet, pierced His side. Jesus had the power to come off The Cross, but He loved us so much that He decided to submit to His Father's will for our freedom. He took the pain without anything to numb it.

We often try to numb the pain with various things. Food, for some, is the number one numbing agent. There are other numbing agents often used, such as drugs and alcohol. We should be careful with our numbing agents to avoid them becoming addictive and adding long-term, lasting negative consequences of unmanaged grief. We can become addicted to anything when we think of consistently depending on anything to number our pain or make us forget it temporarily. God wants us to become addicted to Him. The great news is our addiction to God has eternal positive effects! Yes, Lord!

I didn't become addicted to God until I became sick and tired of consistent pain. I tried to manage my pain without God. Food brought me comfort. As I write, I realize these words are a slap in God's face since I have always said He is my Comforter. "Lord, I pause at this moment and ask you to forgive me. Forgive me for finding comfort in people, places, and things instead of embracing Your painless comfort. I apologize!"

The body of Christ often tries to numb the pain with God. I am a firm believer in God and His ability to do anything but fail. There are things in life that are imperative to deal with and not try to dance and praise over. Grief is one of those things. It's essential not to numb the pain. Lean into the pain and allow yourself to feel what you feel. God will heal the pain. God will bring comfort as only He can.

The things we try to numb the pain with often become our God. Yes, our numbing agents, if not careful, can become idols in our lives. I remember sitting in a therapist's office and him telling me," Carol, I heard your belief in God, but it appears food has become your God." I was upset with him because the truth was hurting. Food had become my God for years. The effect of using food as a numbing agent led to addiction, obesity, hypertension, asthma, sleep apnea, and arthritis.

As I look back on my journey with losses, I wonder what would've happened if I found strength amid pain to grab The Word of God. Have you ever wondered what would have happened if you asked the Lord to help you before forming other gods?

We often experience unnecessary pain due to poor choices. I was told not to make any major decisions within the first six months to a year after death. Often, we are not thinking clearly or are in a mental fog during that time. One of the poor choices I made after the loss of my mother was taking out a large loan. I took the loan out because I decided not to return to work for an extended period.

My place of employment at the time of my mother's death was a huge stimulus for me. My mother worked years at that same place while pregnant with me until her retirement. Many of her co-workers were still employed there at the time of her death. I wasn't ready to return to my place of employment to consistently hear people talking about my mother. I was processing my grief and didn't have the strength to process someone else's grief at the time.

People don't mean any harm by saying certain things and asking questions. What people don't understand is certain words and questions are not helpful. My co-workers would say, "I miss your mother." "She's in a better place." "She was a good worker." "You look just like your mother." I heard all these words and more upon returning to work.

How many times have you heard or said, "they're in a better place?" How is saying that helping anyone experiencing loss? I didn't want to hear my mother was in a better place. I wanted my mother here with me on Earth.

I didn't realize the result of my poor choice of taking a loan to allow me to be off for several months after my mother died would have consequences. Over months the pain intensified, and isolation became real. I didn't necessarily want to be bothered with anyone, not even myself. My pain was real, yet no one understood it. I kept hearing, "you should be over it by now." Someone told me, "Jesus stayed in the grave three days and rose. You should be up by now."

The pain related to my losses caused me to be angry with God. The problem with this emotion was the inability to articulate this with anyone. My being angry with God goes against what I was taught growing up as a child. I was taught never to question God and most certainly don't articulate you're angry with Him. I know this statement may be challenging to accept. It's okay to be angry with God, but don't stay angry. He already knows you're angry with Him. What I love about God is, although we're angry with Him, His love toward us is still unconditional.

The two losses that specifically caused anger was my niece's death and my dad re-marrying 13 years after my mom's death. The anger was associated with the unexpected that I couldn't control. I wish God would've told me that two days before my niece's death would be my last conversation with her. I wish God would have told me that even when my father told me he wasn't going to get married to the person he was briefly dating, he would come back two days later saying he's engaged. I was angry at God - again!

I dealt with my anger incorrectly. Instead of talking to God and asking Him for help, I ran from God and decided I didn't want to talk to Him at all. I behaved like a grown kid throwing a temper tantrum because I wasn't getting my way. I wasn't angry at God! I was angry because I wasn't getting my way. Are you angry at God, or are you angry because things didn't go the way you wanted them to go?

I pray we come to a place where we return to prayer in the midst of our losses. Prayer doesn't have to be filled with fancy words. You honestly may not feel like a lot of words for a moment. It's in these times when it's okay to say, "Lord help me." It's okay to say, "it hurts, and I need you, Lord." Don't be limited by what words to say that you miss the importance of simply praying.

The enemy will have you believe God is angry with you because of your emotions toward Him or God doesn't hear you. Remember *Isaiah 65:24, "and it shall come to pass, that before they call, I will answer, and while they are yet speaking, I will hear."* It's a blessing to know that before we even open our mouths, the Lord already plans to answer us. He may not answer us the way we want Him to answer, but we must trust He knows what's best for us. He is our Creator. The Lord knew us before we were formed in our mother's wombs.

God has not forgotten you in the place of your pain! He sees and knows the pain you're experiencing. God loves us so much that He is consistently standing in the gap for us so that we won't fall. I know the pain is causing you to feel like you're not going to make it. What I love about God not only is *"He able to keep you from falling but to present you faultless before His glory with exceeding joy."* (Jude 24).

We won't always be in pain. *"Many of the afflictions of the righteous, but the Lord delivers us out of them all."* (Psalm 34:19)

The Lord delivers us out of them all I know you're like, "Carol, when am I going to be delivered?" I don't have the answer to that question. I do know that our times are in His hands. (Psalm 31:15).

It may not seem like it, but God is greater than our pain. When the pain is at its most severe, trust the Lord with all your heart and don't lean to your own understanding. In all your ways acknowledge Him knowing that He will direct your path. (Proverbs 3:6) Even in pain, the steps of a good man are ordered by the Lord. (Psalm 37:23) Allow God to reign in the midst of your pain. You may not see it now or understand it, but great gain is coming out of this pain.

Although our journey is different, I know the pain of loss can be great. The pain of my first Mother's Day after my mom's death was excruciating. The pain was so great I even asked the Lord to take me home. Distraught, I eventually fell asleep and woke up the next morning. I was upset with the Lord for not honoring my request. The Lord didn't honor my request because He had a greater purpose and plan for my life. We don't always like or understand God's purpose and plan for our lives. However, once we seriously embrace God's purpose and plan, it will decrease of pain, frustration, and anxiety. All these emotions are often a result of us resisting God. We don't like to hear it, but our purpose can be birthed from pain.

Chapter 2

Losses

When we think about loss, we tend to think of loss related to the death of a loved one. You will discover in this chapter loss is not just related to the death of a loved one. There are many distinct types of losses, all of which can cause individuals to experience grief.

We never understand loss, let alone grief. We must trust God in the process and allow Him to be God. I am struggling writing this book. I know this is my Kingdom assignment on Earth. I kid you not; the moment I said, yes to penning these words, the loss started intensifying. I am currently writing on the plane to attend the funeral of my first cousin, my father's nephew. Alvin died two days after my first cousin Helena died. Helena is my mom's niece.

The pain of loss can do a sneak attack. My cousin Helena loved her aunt Josephine. I can hear her now, "Carol, how is Aunt Jo!" It didn't surprise me that her daughter Kyia found a picture of my mother. I just wasn't prepared to receive it via text. I was working when the picture of my mother arrived. I had never seen that picture of her. The pain that gripped my heart was unbelievable. Tears streamed down my face as I asked the Lord for relief. The image produced a roller coaster of emotions. It was one of few pictures of my mother in her fullness; before entering the hospital in 2006.

I was stuck in grief for years after my mother died. I commented to myself that I would do everything necessary not ever to be stuck again. It's one reason I enjoyed reading Sabria Mathis's book *Unstuck*. I knew I had to allow myself the moment but not stay there. I had to lean into a pain that snuck up on me. Yes, I had to allow myself to feel what I was feeling to experience relief. The cry was just what the doctor ordered. The release of my tears at that moment didn't take anything away from me as a person. It was more liberating than holding them in and losing the inability to function from the bottled-up pain of the moment.

Loss can cause you the opportunity to miss love. When we lose something, it feels like a piece of ourselves has left. We can never replace the loss and shouldn't try to. We can gain during loss. We can gain a greater appreciation of God's love amid loss. A greater gain of love for ourselves and a greater gain of love for others is possible. There are times when we struggle with loving ourselves because, honestly, we don't know who we are. Our identity, when wrapped up in our loss, becomes a struggle to understand self.

All my life, I did my best to live like my mother wanted me to live. Yes, rebellious, but the focus was always to make her proud whether she thought so or not. It was so terrible that I felt trapped. I never knew the importance of creating my own identity. I never even thought that my identity was important. What is your identity?

Parents, it's important you begin telling your child at an early age who they are and who God says they are. Allow them to develop their own identity with your coaching. As they grow up, they will be okay being who they are and not what or who you want them to be or try to be someone else. You plant the identity seed. Identity planting is essential. It allows the authentic self to be manifested amid loss because it was always present before the loss.

Loss may cause loneliness; but loneliness has a purpose. You will never be able to discover your true authentic self unless you spend time with yourself. Validate yourself.

Loss can abort purpose. The enemy causes you to take your focus off your purpose during grief.

The enemy can use the loss to distract you from moving in your already assigned purpose, while distorting the truth that there is more to your life. Pray the scales are removed from your eyes so you can see your purpose before the foundation of the world and your current purpose. Declare and decree, "I will see my purpose, walk in purpose, and fulfill the God-given purpose for my life."

Your purpose is to live and love. Your purpose is to bear and produce fruit. You are a dominator. Dominate according to God's will, purpose, and plan. Ask the Lord to show you your purpose in the Kingdom despite the loss.

Loss can often cause the feeling of diminished love from others and the inability to love again. God is love and He desires to love us even as we grieve a loss. God's presence does make the difference and feel the void in the loss. Liberty will happen for the grieving. Let's remove the grave clothes. We can become so familiar with loss that it's all we know, and it quickly becomes our identity. Let's remove barriers that keep us bound. These barriers are thoughts, people, and things. The enemy doesn't want us or anyone free in their minds. We become free when we immediately dismiss the lie of the enemy with God's Word.

Lie: We will never make it through this.

Truth: We can do all things through Christ who strengthens us.

We will swim on broken pieces.

Lie: We can't live without the loss.

Truth: We will live and not die to declare the work of the Lord in the land of the living

The Lord satisfies us with long life. The Lord came to give us life and that more abundantly.

Lie: We are alone.

Truth: The Lord will never leave us nor forsake us. God's Word overpowers every lie of the enemy. Let's choose to believe God's Word and not the lies of the enemy.

Loss requires getting in the Lord's presence, His Word is to release His power to endure until deliverance comes. Endure because, during loss, God does want to reveal lessons. God wants to show you first who He is. Experiences are the best teacher. Think about it. How can you say healing has taken place if you've never been sick?

Life does happen despite the loss. Loss is never the end. The Lord is with you! If you want to gain, a loss is often part of the process. Look at Christ's life. He chose to lose His life so that He could gain souls. He had to lose His life so that we could experience life. A seed must first be buried to be planted; then, after it's planted, work must be done to support the seed becoming new life as something else. John 12:24 (NIV) says: *"Very truly I tell you, unless a kernel of wheat falls to the ground and dies, it remains only a single seed. But if it dies, it produces many seeds."* Legacies are seeds planted. The seeds planted must be tended to and nurtured to bring a harvest. We are the water for the seed/legacy cultivated.

There's a change in the midst of loss. The enemy works hard to convince us that change is bad. There are times where loss is ordained to promote refashioning. The enemy works hard to convince us that change is bad. My dad is elderly with health challenges. When my mother died, I told the Lord I didn't want to be a caregiver for another parent or bury another parent. Years after my mother died, I returned home to live with my father to ensure he would be okay with my mother's death. While there, I began to ask the Lord for help because I was shying away from ministering. I didn't feel comfortable traveling or even leaving him alone for extended times. I remember my niece telling me, "Carol, the Lord is going to send you help."

The Lord sent help through a stepmother. The Lord may not send us what we want in the way we want, but He is God and knows what we need beyond our human understanding. We must embrace His way of choosing to answer our prayers according to His will, purpose, and plan for our lives.

God is Jehovah Jireh (the God who provides) during loss. I became a Registered Nurse in May 1997. I never thought I would become unemployed with that type of licensure and experience.

Well, to my surprise, on September 2, 2011, I lost my job. It was unexpected. God as Jehovah Jireh is not limited to supplying money. God provided not only preparation but guidance. There comes a time where we should listen to the small still voice giving us directions and instructions. The Lord is our guide. I called my friend and asked her to bring any message from Pastor Creflo Dollar, of World Changers Church International, in Atlanta, Georgia. Pastor Dollar preached in one of his messages, "if someone gives you a pink slip, you should bless the Lord." I admit, after hearing those words, I thought, how do you bless the Lord when receiving a pink slip? When I received the long, legal white envelope with my termination letter, I couldn't bless the Lord. However, I was grateful the Lord prepared me.

Trust God even when you don't know the outcome. While traveling to the subway station, "I Trust You" by gospel artist James Fortune was playing on the radio. I've heard this song numerous times, but it was like the singer was in my car that day feeding those words to me. When I got to work, I felt led to clean out my desk. Cleaning out my desk was the opposite of my routine, but God said clean off and out your desk, so that's what I did. My usual morning routine was to gather my patients' census, review the number of new admissions at my assigned facility, and determine how many patients I had to call for concurrent reviews. Then I would start work.

I didn't realize the Lord was even preparing me by changing my lunchtime. I went to lunch every day at two P.M. This particular day, I left the office at 11:30 to grab lunch at Potbelly, known for their submarine sandwiches. I brought my lunch back to the office and ate. I had no idea I would be one of the individuals laid off that afternoon. I was working at my desk when my friend, a manager, called me to her office. The look on her face showed this was not going to be a casual conversation. She asked me to have a seat, handed me a legal-size white envelope, and said, "Carol, you no longer have a job."

The Lord prepared me! When she handed the envelope to me and spoke, I was not my usual vocal self. I was calm and said nothing. My response puzzled her. She continued, "Please get your things together quickly; because they are sending security at two o'clock to escort people out of the building."

The company I was working for decided to lay off seventeen people. I was baffled. I had never been late. I received a great evaluation. I practiced excellent work ethics. Why was this happening to me? The way the company managed the situation was painful. God knew the company was getting ready to close. Jehovah Garash (the God of the way out) orchestrated the exit before shutting down.

Monday, November 9, 2020, I was taking a nap; around 8:00 P.M., I heard a noise coming from the roof. It sounded like someone was breaking into the house through the ceiling. I changed my position in the bed, not overly concerned. Moments later, I heard the same sound but this time louder. I decided to get up. The moment I stood up, the entire ceiling fell, debris and items in the attic crashed atop me. I was grateful my roommates were home and heard the crash. The debris had me trapped in the room. They were able to force the door open and get me out.

I sustained only a shoulder injury, which is miraculous. It's amazing how things happen to help us recognize God's ability to protect. The triage nurse asked me what happened. While I explained, I also showed her pictures on my phone of the aftermath. Shocked, she then showed others in the emergency room and said, "Jesus! You're blessed to be alive without sustaining any other injuries."

The Lord kept me alive to tell you that even though the loss may be significant, and you don't know the result, He has you and is working things out!

There was insulation and debris everywhere in my room. I was unable to decide if any clothes were salvageable. But I had placed clothes in the dryer earlier that day and forgot to take them out, those items were the only clothes I had for a week. I smile now as I think about how God supplied clothing from a dryer and new clothing in the strangest of incidents.

I had no idea the loss was a setup for better in so many ways. I am grateful for friends. Three of my friends came and packed up what was still good. My best friend allowed me to stay at her place until the completion of repairs without charging me anything. I decided not to return to the former house when God opened a door for me to move into a fully furnished home without significant rent changes. Plus, people unexpectedly gave me money during this time. I reaped seeds sown! A loss will manifest the seeds you've sown. Yes, it will!

Everyone around suggested I should file a lawsuit. I must admit it came to my mind; I had reasons to pursue legal action. Months prior to the incident there was a leak in the house and the landlord sent someone to repair it. I had been noticing a lengthy line in the ceiling above my head, so I asked the repairman his thoughts. He discovered there was a mountain of items in the attic pushing the ceiling down. The repairman told me, "If you don't get this fix the ceiling is going to fall on your head." I told the landlord what I was told; he assured me he was going to have it fixed. That never happened. Although, the night of the incident, he did ask, "Why didn't you remind me to get it fixed?"

It's imperative in all situations to obey the Lord even when it doesn't make sense. The Lord will reward you for your obedience. The Lord told me not to sue, and even though I heard Him, I started reaching out to assess the process and the possibility of winning. I finally submitted totally to the Lord. I received a call two weeks later from my supervisor, "Carol, I thought you would want to know they gave the nurses a raise." Then after receiving a raise, the CEO decided to give all employees a bonus. I received another raise four months later! I appreciated all the Lord blessed me with and honestly wasn't expecting another raise anytime soon. I passionately believe because I obeyed the Lord and did not file legal action against my landlord, I was blessed abundantly. Obedience may not make sense, but God rewards it. This loss drew me closer to God because I got to see who He is on a greater level.

We talked about grief experiences not being only related to the loss of a loved one. Let's continue our journey together as I share my experience with the grief associated with the loss of relationships. We will start with one of the most significant losses. November 17, 2006, my mother went home to be with the Lord! I don't ever recall this type of pain with any of the losses that occurred. The Lord prepared me for my mother's death. I had a dream in 2002, where I saw my mother in a casket. The dream was so real, as if the casket was in front of me. I called a close friend and shared the dream. They informed me mother wasn't getting ready to die, but I needed to work on our relationship because something is getting ready to happen.

I took her advice. I had to humble myself in the areas where I thought I was right for being angry and bitter at my mother for not validating me as a child and only teaching me the ways of God and not teaching me how to live a balanced life. I also finally shared the molestation with my mother and father. It didn't go well with my mother. My mother said, "Okay. Children do things to each other." I ran upstairs and cried. I could hear my father scolding her, "Josephine, why would you say that to Carol? You couldn't tell Carol was hurt by these incidents?" Even after being hurt again by my mother, I had to push past the hurt and heal our relationship. It was clear something was happening. The Lord gave us one year of creating a healthier mother-daughter relationship; while I'm glad we had that mending season, I still mourn the fact that we didn't have a loving, engaged relationship over the years. There was the lingering question for me. Why was I only allowed to have a healthy relationship with my mother when her death was pending, when my sister and even my friends had healthy relationships with their mothers for years? I still, after fifteen years, haven't received the answer. God knows I keep the spirit of jealousy under prayer. It's not easy to see others experience a joyous mother-daughter relationship while I was only afforded one year.

After the year was over, mother's health significantly declined. My mother could cook! I didn't become full-figured by staring at food. Her signature meal was fried chicken, turkey, homemade dressing, and pound cake. As she declined, however, she started burning everything she cooked. I also noticed a change in her memory. I made an appointment for her to see her primary doctor, who referred us to a neurologist. The appointment was September 20, 2003, the day of Hurricane Isabel. I had no idea I was being prepared for a storm in my world.

The neurologist began to ask my mother a series of questions to evaluate her short and long-term memory. I was sitting there holding back tears. My mother never struggled with counting or remembering anything you told her, but that was different during the evaluation.

Her diagnosis - Alzheimer's/Dementia. As we left the office, the wind and rain from Hurricane Isabel had picked up. What was I going to do? I found the strength to share the diagnosis with the family, and that didn't go well. My father and my sister didn't believe my mother had Alzheimer's/ Dementia. I also had to walk a fine line with my dad. Because he was the spouse, decision-making authority rested with him. I had to be fully aware and ever prepared to advocate and ask questions yet defer decisions to him.

While at work one day, I get a call from a car salesman. He told me my mother bought a car from him. I called my sister and told her what happened, and she yelled, "Who let her go buy a car?" I had no idea. I knew my mother had no business driving. I told my sister and my father. The only thing I could do was pray that the Lord keep her safe. Well, my mother did have one accident. One would think the accident would be enough even though it wasn't her fault.

Unfortunately, the accident didn't get my family members' attention; nor did it call for my dad taking the keys. On another occasion, my mother went to the bank alone. Fortunately, the Lord had my cousin be in the bank. She was able to call my dad and tell him she had locked the keys in a running car. When my dad got to the bank and unlocked the car, he told us the radio was blasting.

Then, my dad realized driving a car was no longer a possibility for my mother. The next problem arose when we realize my mother could not stay home alone. My father was working a full-time job, and I was working a full-time job as well. Well, everyone again thought my mother was fine. Again, all I could do was pray. I was working the night shift, and on my way home from work, I received a call from the secretary at the job who told me, "Carol, the police picked up your mother, and she's at your neighbor's house." My mother had left home, in the winter cold, without a coat. She forgot the coat, but she didn't forget her purse. My mom never forgot to have her purse with her. The Lord protected my mother. A lady saw my mother walking, pulled over, and called the police. The lady also gave my mother her daughter's coat. The police had come to the house, but I wasn't there at the time. My neighbor happened to be outside and allowed her to stay there until I got home. Later, the lady who called the police stopped by the house to check on my mother and brought her lunch. She asked if it was okay for her to have it. We thanked her! My dad and I eventually found a caregiver to come in while we were at work. We had multiple incidents that kept us on our toes. We're grateful the Lord covered my mother every time.

Three years later, my mother suddenly started falling often for no clear reason. She was admitted for tests and observation, and despite my family's urging me to leave and get some rest, I stayed with her nightly. I wanted to make sure she was safe. She started to decline while hospitalized and one Tuesday decided to stop eating. She said, "I am ready to go home!" I knew what she meant but brushed it off, telling her, "You can't go home now."

My mother had always informed me that she didn't want any tubes in her. I told my father my mother's wishes based on conversations prior to dementia. We honored her request. Due to her not eating, she became worse. The hospital could no longer to treat her there, because her case had become custodial care. My father and I were asked to look at nursing homes. The nursing homes were expensive, and my dad never wanted to place my mother in one. My dad's thoughts were to take my mother home. I was not sure how we would manage my mother at home with the finality of her health. The next day, a case manager asked why we were considering a nursing home versus hospice. I wasn't quite sure my dad or family was ready to prepare for the death of my mother. The case manager explained hospice to my father. I explained it again to make sure he understood. The case manager informed us the insurance would pay 100% for inpatient hospice and asked us to visit a facility called the Washington Home.

As I walked into the Washington Home, I couldn't believe my eyes. The facility was gorgeous. It was like being in your own home. The rooms were fully furnished with lovely furniture for the patient and a pull-out sofa for the family member. There was closet space and a nice bathroom. They had a separate kitchen area with tables, and there was also a lounge with a television, books, etc. My dad and I agreed it was the perfect place for my mother.

November 7, 2006, my mother was transferred to the Washington Home. The staff provided excellent care to my mother, dad, and myself. I stayed there with my mother. When the staff came and checked on her, they checked to make sure I was okay.

Each day she was getting closer to her transition. I remember one morning the staff was turning her, and mother said, "Hey, Ardell." The staff member said to me in a joking manner, "Don't you see Ardell?" I told her, "You and mother may see Ardell, but I don't see Ardell." I knew the end was coming closer. I've been told when people start seeing their dead loved ones, it's a sign of transition.

I didn't struggle with my mother's transitioning because I remembered the dream of her in a casket. My family, on the other hand, was different, particularly my sister. When my sister would come to see our mother in hospice, she was expecting a Lazarus moment. When I left, I told the nurse my sister was on her way, and she was going to come praying, trying to raise our mother like Lazarus. When I came back, the nurses smiled and said, "You know your sister." My sister had faith until the end. I wasn't knocking her faith, but I had already been prepared for my mother's transition.

Even when the Lord prepares you for death, it still isn't easy. I was having lunch with Co-Pastor Veda McCoy, Judah Christian Center, at a restaurant in Washington DC. I can't remember the name of the restaurant, but I had a Reuben sandwich with French fries fried hard. As Co-Pastor and I were talking, I said, "Co-Pastor, my mother is going to die today." All she could respond was, "Oh boy!" We spent the afternoon talking about my intuition concerning death.

When I get back to hospice, my dad was preparing to leave. I was so sure it was the day of my mother's death. I didn't want my father to go home. I said, dad, "No, don't leave; let me order us some dinner." I ordered Chinese food. We were sitting eating when my phone rang. It was one of my dearest friends Nicole Jenkins. Nicole was with me through the very beginning of my mother's journey with Alzheimer's. Nicole listened to me talk and cry. She allowed me to be human during the entire process. I talked to Nicole for a few moments and told her I would check on my mother and call her back.

I entered my mother's room and noticed her chest was not moving. I checked again and saw no rising and falling of her chest. She was dead. I went to the nurse's station and told them she was gone. The nurse said," Your mother isn't dead. We just left her room and changed her position." She got up and came into the room, noticed no rise, and fall of her chest, and looked for a pulse. She confirmed what I had already told her. I told the nurse I knew my mother would try to leave when I wasn't present. It was my desire to be present when she transitioned. The nurse said she believed my mother heard my footsteps crossing the threshold and died seconds before entering the room because she didn't want me there when she transitioned. I also believe God didn't want me there either.

The tasks then became relaying the news to my father, family, and friends. I called my sister and softly said, "Jean mom is dead." My sister replied, "Carol, who pronounced her dead? Did you?" I said again, "Jean, mother is dead." My sister still was trying to figure out who said she was dead. My father yelled, "Carol, you told her three times Josephine was dead, now hang up the phone." I obeyed my father and hung up the phone. My dad left the room as I laid my head on my mother's chest crying. I called my brother/friend Nathan and told him. I am not even sure how Nathan got to the hospice facility so quickly.

I appreciate him getting there so fast! I tell you, he's an angel sent from God always in a time of need. While Nathan was there, the funeral home came to pick up the body. The person who came looked very morbid in her black. As she got the bag out, I told her I would place my mother in the bag. I figured I'd done this so many times; I could at least do it for my mother. I was surprised Nathan helped me without my asking. We placed her in the bag and started zipping it. As we get to her neck, the funeral person placed her hand on my hand, "Stop!" I wasn't sure why she wanted me to stop? She explained, "Most people struggle with zipping the back completely." I assured her that wasn't a problem for me.

Once I was back at my mother's house, the phone rang off the hook, people were dropping in, and the community mourning was underway. We still needed to tell my niece her grandmother had died. Repeatedly, in her denial, she said, "My grandmother is not dead." At that moment, it was Nathan who put a smile on my face through pain and tears. Nathan said as we stepped outside for fresh air, "Carol, if your mother isn't dead, me and you surely are going to jail because we just wrapped a live body."

As we made the funeral home arrangements, I paused in disbelief as we stepped into the room with the caskets, I gasped laying my hand on one casket, "Dad, this is the casket." My dad just looked! It took us both back to a dream I had. The dream, years before my mother's transition, showed me the exact casket standing before us. In it, I saw my mother lying in a white casket lined with a white quilt. She had on a white suit with a light pink blouse.

I dealt with my family's moments of denial, until denial hit me! I felt like I was in a bad dream waiting for someone to wake me up! I had it bad! The funeral home did an impressive job preparing my mother's body, with one exception. They had my mother's hands crossed, and a beautiful handkerchief was placed in them. Well, when I went to view the body, one of her hands dropped. I exclaimed, "See, I told you my mother wasn't dead." The funeral home attendant explained," Ms. Williams, we apologize; the glue came undone." I said, "You all need to fix this because you all will scare someone to death." It took me weeks to accept my mother was dead. I told my dad I wanted to go to the cemetery and dig up the grave. My dad said, "Carol, you're talking crazy; go right ahead and go to the cemetery and dig up the grave. You're going to jail." That quickly snapped me back to reality!

The day of my mother's funeral arrived, Monday, November 27, 2006. I had all kinds of mixed emotions. I wanted to get everything over with. The first thing that happened took God to keep me from speaking in unknown tongues as Carol was about to give utterance. A former co-worker of my mother called who was known to have a drinking problem. It was clear in hearing her speech she was drunk. She slurred, "You didn't tell me your mother was sick. I just found out not only was she sick but dead." She then yelled, "You should've told me." She then started crying. I removed the phone from my ear, thinking She had lost her mind. I hung up the phone! It wasn't the day to deal with it. I decided I need to do something to help me quickly before leaving the house. I wrote my first poem entitled "Pain." I published the poem in my book *A Seed for A Day God's Word Producing Productivity*.

I told my family I wanted to close the casket. They believed I had done enough and wouldn't be able to handle it. They were right. I convinced them at least let me do a tribute. My nephew, always a jokester, said, "Okay, go right ahead, but if you get up there and start crying and falling out, no one is coming to pick you up!" I felt the Lord was going to give me strength, and He did provide me with strength.

Everyone's experience is different! The hardest part for me that day was leaving the gravesite. I was in a daze, a friend had to come to get me because people wanted to speak, and the family had already gotten into the limo to return to the repast. I felt like this was the finale.

When my mother died, I became stuck in grief for years. I was functional in public to those who didn't know the hurting Carol. However, privately, I was a mess. I went to work, came home, laid down, and cried myself to sleep. I took a leave of absence when my mother died. Well, it turned into an extended vacation. I went to church because it was instilled in me.

Although going to church, I had beef with God. Growing up, I was taught you don't ever question God. Well, I had questions. "God, even though you warned me, why didn't you tell me it would be so painful? Why didn't you allow me to have more time before her death? God, just why?" Although I was taught Sundays were for church, Mother's Day was not up for discussion. I wasn't going to church on Mothers' Day.

The death of my mother taught me time doesn't heal all wounds. Yes, God is a healer. However, we must take part in our healing process by incorporating grief work. I also learned that you shouldn't grieve without God. I know some may disagree with this statement. I can't tell you how often I've heard not to mention God during grief because it's offering people false hope. Well, let me pause and stand on my belief in God, the God of hope. I realized I did live a hopeless life because I did not include God I knew in a difficult season in my life.

You don't like where you are in life. You're angry with God. You're tired of the losses you've experienced. Don't try to keep going in this season of your life without God. God is the God of hope! He is the God of hope! Even when you're angry with Him, He will remain consistent in His character. God staying consistent even when we're angry with Him is what makes Him different from people.

Leaving God out of my grief led to hopelessness and even thoughts of suicide! I remembered on Mother's Day attending church, then returning home to end my life. I had enough! I wanted out! I remember Bishop Greg Dennis preached a powerful message. God was using Him to speak directly to me. I was at the altar with others when I felt something started to break. However, I was aware of surroundings and noticed everyone was going back to their seat. Church was over, and I was about to leave. Another one of my dearest friends, Dr. Toni Boulware Stackhouse, came walking fast with this puzzled look as she spoke to someone to get my attention, "Pastor Tonya Dennis, Kingdom Worship Center, told me to catch Carol before she leaves; we need to pray for her." Toni's look was like what is wrong, and why didn't you tell me something was wrong. As I entered the room, I noticed Overseer Lois Anderson, also of Kingdom Worship Center. Pastor Tonya says," Carol, you're not going home to end your life. It's all on you."

I was in a daze! I knew God was yet again blocking my death. She said we're going to pray. She started to pray and then had to leave. Overseer Louis and Dr. Toni stayed there and prayed me through. I remember being on the floor curled up crying. Overseer Louis was right there on the floor with her hands on my back, praying. She didn't get up until I got up. When I tell you, I left knowing the chains were broken. I've attended church on Mother's Day since then. I never served in any capacity on that day until Mother's Day 2021, but at least God freed me to get to church on Mother's Day.

I will always appreciate those three ladies because they obeyed God, and my life has forever changed. When God shows us something we may not necessarily want to deal with, obey God; you never know whether the person's life depends on it.

The moment I started moving toward not allowing grief to be my identity, allowing God to be God during grief and not trying to do grief without Him and adding grief work - I began to become unstuck!

You don't have to be stuck in grief! It's not God's design or plan for your life! God wants you to identify with who He says you are. Grief is just a symptom of the pain of loss; it's not who you are! You're fearfully and wonderfully made even in grief! Yes, you are! You're accepted in The beloved! He sees you as the apple of His eye! He loves you! He loves all aspects of you! Include God on your journey! Understand that He is a lamp unto your feet and a light unto your path. He is always with you! He's always fighting for you! He's never lost a fight. Yes, grief is not too hard for Him!

It's essential to include grief work! It could be as simple as journaling your emotions or thoughts. Join a support group. It's okay to seek professional help! There are tools to help you do the work. You're more than welcome to reach out to me by visiting www.caresolutions.website

The death of my Aunt Eula, my dad's sister, was painful. We would travel to Atlanta every year for a substantial part of my life. I would talk to my aunt at least once a week. I loved my Aunt

Eula! She was the semblance of a mother-daughter relationship my mother couldn't provide. I talked to my aunt about any and everything.

My aunt was another cheerleader of my ministry. When her son was found dead in his home, she asked me to do the eulogy. My aunt had faith in me! I had never done a eulogy. However, I had my black manual (*The Star Book for Ministers* by Edward T. Hiscox). I rely on God and my manual. The original plan was I was to do the eulogy only; somehow, I ended up officiating as well. The pastor scheduled to do it was late. He came strolling down the aisle like he was on time. I thought since he's late surely, he was going to do the committal. He didn't.

On the day of my cousin's funeral, I learned something I never knew. I have attended many funerals and watched the preacher, or the funeral home attendant say, "ashes to ashes and dust to dust." They would then make a cross on the casket. I never knew the cross marking was made where the person's head was facing. Upon getting to the gravesite, the funeral attendant helped me out of the car, and while they were getting the casket out of the hearse, the driver advised, "Pastor, the head is this way." I followed his lead the entire time, looking like I knew what was happening. It taught me for future reference to always ask which direction was the head.

When my aunt's husband passed, she called me again to do the eulogy. I love my aunt, but being her personal eulogist was not what I signed up for. The Lord yet again was my strength. I had to do both eulogies while dealing with my grief and memories.

My dad and my aunt were close and would talk every day. My aunt called my dad on a Sunday evening and said, "Robert, I am going to call you right back." She would always call back within an hour when she said that. Well, instead of her calling back, my cousin called. My aunt had a heart attack, and the prognosis wasn't good. My dad and I headed to Atlanta the next day.

When I got to the hospital, my aunt was in ICU on life support. She was alert, oriented and was able to understand everything happening. My aunt and I had a conversation years ago concerning health; based on the conversation, I knew what my aunt wanted. So, I asked her, "You don't want all these tubes, do you?" She shook her head no. Unfortunately, there was nothing I could do because her son was the next of kin. He wasn't in any shape to manage any affairs, even before my aunt became sick.

My cousins all came up from Alabama to see my aunt while she was in the hospital. My death intuition kicked in again. One of my cousins asked that we pray and asked that I lead the petition before God. I thought she was kidding. I was about to fall apart. At that moment, I had to be productive in the midst of my emotional pain. I began to pray with tears streaming down my face. I realized that would be the last time I will see my aunt alive. She wrote on a pad, "Take care of Earl!" Earl was her son. My dad and I headed back home. On the drive, I told my dad, "Aunt Eula is going to die before we get back home." We were home less than an hour when my cousin called to announce her death.

Sometimes moving and being productive through grief is quite painful. I knew the Lord prepared me for my aunt's death because I would have to manage my emotions and support my dad and cousins. I was helping in planning a funeral from home until my dad, and I could get back to Atlanta. One of the first things my cousin asked was, "Carol, you're doing the eulogy, correct?" I told him, "As much as I know Aunt Eula would want me to do her eulogy, I can't. I will do anything else." We agreed I would do the prayer of comfort.

My dad and I got to Atlanta to help complete the funeral arrangements. I was sitting in the funeral home, doing my best to hold it together. You talk about memories, on top of not liking the feeling of funeral homes.

The day of my aunt's funeral arrived! I sat next to my father during the service, supporting him. Suddenly I started bouncing my right leg up and down. My dad kept tapping me and telling me to stop. I honestly tried. Whenever I am incredibly nervous, my legs shake. However, I'd never had an experience like that. Once they called my name to do the prayer of comfort, my leg shook more. The Lord helped the kid out though, and I prayed without my leg giving way under me.

Once, we were all back at my aunt's house. One of my cousins told me, "I enjoyed your prayer. I was glad when it was over because, before the prayer, I honestly thought you were going to stomp a hole in the floor the way your leg was shaking."

Praying during that moment was a testament to not allowing grief to leave me paralyzed. I had to move beyond my comfort zone and emotions.

I don't know if you have ever experienced the loss of a best friend. I have. My best friend Barbara Lawrence Harrison went home to be with the Lord on October 4, 2005. She died 13 months before my mother. I was often told that Barbara and I looked alike. We often dressed in the same style outfits with different colors.

Barbara's greatest desire was to be married to the man she knew God had designed for her. I am so glad the Lord gave her heart's desire. I was supposed to be a part of the bridal party, but unfortunately, I was I a leg cast and using a walker. I did attend the beautiful wedding. Brian Harrison loved and cared for Barbara until she died of breast cancer.

Barbara had moved to Myrtle Beach, South Carolina. I would talk to her almost every day to make sure she was okay. I would read the Bible and pray with her. I thought I was doing something small. Until she told me, "Thank you so much for reading the Bible and praying with me. Carol, people don't know sometimes the pain is so great. I can't sit up to read the Bible and pray like I want to pray." I will always remember those words because it's the small things that means the most to people at times.

I will never forget my last visit with my best friend which was the last time seeing her alive. We had a ball that day at the mall in Myrtle Beach. Brian was wheeling her around the mall when we saw our favorite store, Lane Bryant. I told Brian we had to go in the store. That meant it became my turn to become the driver. Barbara and I looked around, finally deciding on matching pajama sets. I still have the pajama pants.

Barbara wanted me to go with her to her radiology treatment appointment. It was at the radiology appointment I noticed the strength of my friend and her faith. You could tell she was in a lot of pain, but she never complained. She always said, "I am going live and not die to declare the works of the Lord in the land of the living." Barbara touched the lives of her healthcare professionals. The staff at the radiology appointment praised Barbara for how she was managing her treatment. Barbara was letting her light shine in a dark place.

When Sheryl, Barbara's sister called me on October 4, 2005, and told me Barbara was dead, I was numb. My best friend was dead. The person who prayed for and with me. The person who knew the hand of the Lord was on my life. The person who told me, "Don't be bitter; God has better." The person who would play my keyboard and we would sing "I Really Love the Lord" together. The person who consistently said, "I shall live and not die to declare the works of the Lord in the land of the living." Barbara Lawrence Harrison was gone home to be with the Lord! I had a moment of angst with God. I yelled, "What did I miss? Barbara had faith and trusted You to the end. I joined my faith with Barbara's. I did not doubt you would heal her. What in the world happened?"

Attending Barbara's Homegoing Service didn't seem possible. I wasn't sure how I was going to get there. I wasn't sure who my support was going to be for this hard place. My brother/friend Nathan comes to the rescue again. He drove me to and from South Carolina. I am not even quite sure how we got to Myrtle Beach so fast. We got there on Sunday for the Pre-Homegoing Service and came back home the next day.

The family asked me to do a tribute to my best friend. I don't know where my mind was when they were giving me instructions. I thought my tribute was supposed to be during Sunday Service, that's what I was prepared to do. I get to the pre-homegoing service, walk down the aisle to view the body, with Nathan by my side, and I see my best friend lying there looking like an African American doll. It took me a few moments to get myself together. I sat there for a while, before wondering why I hadn't been called to give the remarks. Maureen, one of Barbara's sisters, corrected me, "Carol, no, you're on the program at the homegoing service to do a tribute."

The Lord gave me a clear picture of death on the day of that service. Barbara's Pastor remarked," I know some of you are struggling with God based on Barbara always saying, she's going to live and not die to declare the works of the Lord. Well, Barbara is living. She's now living with the Lord in a new body. Barbara is free from pain." I admit it's not what I wanted to hear at the moment. I wanted Barbara to live here on Earth. However, after seeing my best friend in the pain she was enduring and even hearing the pain in her voice when talking, I am glad she's living in a new pain-free body. We didn't like the way God answered our prayers! However, He is a prayer-answering God according to His will and purpose.

I will always remember and love my best friend. I keep her memory alive each year by at least doing a Facebook tribute to her on October 4th and on her birthday October 30th. "Barbara, thank you for your unconditional love, support, and prayers. I know you would be so proud of me in this season of my life. I know you're looking down cheering for me!"

The death of my niece rocked my world but pushed me right into purpose! I was getting my hair done on September 3, 2016, when I received a call from nephew, "Carol, Teza is dead!" My nephew is a jokester, so you never know when he's serious. However, I wasn't sure about his words. He placed his wife on the phone, and she confirmed his words, "Carol, Teza is dead!" I started yelling at the top of my lungs with tears streaming down my face. I was holding the phone. My friend Wendy came running down the stairs, I asked her to take the phone and ask them to repeat what they told me. My niece was dead. Lord, what I am going to do now? I started thinking of all that needed to be done while I was getting my hair finished. I was not sure how my dad was going to take the news because he loved his granddaughter and God knows she loved her granddad; so, I asked that no one tell him anything until I and his fiancé' spoke with him.

When I got in the car, I called my dearest friend Angie and told her my niece had died. She did well for my purpose, but I know it bothered her. My niece was loved by everyone she met. As I was talking to her, it occurred to me that I had no idea how to get to my dad's house. I couldn't think of how to get there. I had to place the address in my GPS. I told him the news and he broke down crying.

My dad's wedding was planned for Friday, September 9, 2016. What in the world was the next step? It was too much to think about my dad's wedding and my niece's death. My immediate thought was getting to my sister. We were packed and on the road in hours. I wanted to lay eyes on my sister and make sure she was okay. I wound up doing more than laying eyes on my sister. My sister and my nephew came and picked me up from the hotel. We went to my niece's house to get things for her body.

My sister had planned my niece's homegoing service for Saturday, September 10, 2016. My dad and his fiancé decided to still have the wedding on Friday, September 9, 2016, but to cancel the reception and get on the road early Saturday morning. I originally was going back with them since I was one of the bridesmaids in the wedding. That changed when my sister broke down in tears and exclaimed, she didn't know what she was going to do. My heart was broken As fate would have it, I was already off for the week. Rather than go back for the wedding, I stayed with my sister and did all I could do to help.

I was so busy being a support to my sister, I never had a moment to deal with my emotions. Well, it hit me hard the day of my dad's wedding, Friday, September 9, 2016. My cousin came from Atlanta to attend my dad's wedding. They didn't mean any harm by sending me a picture of my dad and stepmother after the wedding. I looked at the picture and started yelling and crying. I remember Aunt Pumpkin coming in the room to comfort me. My phone rang and Angie was checking on me. I tried to talk and started crying again. It dawned on me, in a week I lost my niece who was like a sister to me and my father who is now marrying another woman who looks and has so many similar ways of my mother. The pain of it all came down on me and it was too much to bear.

Although the emotions and the pain were hard to bear, I couldn't stay in that place of crying and yelling. I had to help my sister with the completion of things. Aunt Carlene and I worked together on the program for my niece's homegoing service. I wrote a poem that described my niece called, "Classy Lady". I featured it as a dedication in my book, *A Seed for A Day - God's Word Producing Productivity*.

My niece's life spoke for her! There were so many people at my niece's service that Cheraw, South Carolina, was shut down! People came from far and near. The sanctuary was full, and the overflow was full. I appreciate my friends who traveled to support me. They were a fantastic support to me as I bore the responsibility of being strong for everyone else. I then saw my brother/friend Nathan and his mother being ushered to their seats. The final viewing of the body was hard for me. I don't remember much except someone helping me out the front door and Nathan coming to help me.

My niece's death strangely was the backdrop for a potential romantic hook-up. I was with my sister at the funeral home, viewing the body. The funeral home director told her, "Pastor Jean, I think I am in love with your sister." My sister looked at him crazy and asked, "Oh, you're in love with my sister?" He later came to the house, and Aunt Pumpkin, being a matchmaker, stepped into the mix. He asked me out on a date. We scheduled the date for the Monday after the funeral. I will say when it came to making sure I was okay at the funeral and the graveside, he took care of me.

One would have thought I was getting married on that Monday! My sister was funny, "Carol, let me see what you're wearing. What shoes are you going to wear? Here's some perfume." When I got dressed, she demanded, "Carol, let me see how you look. Oh, you look nice." Then, I heard the doorbell ring. It was my dad and my stepmother. Lord, not the family at the house like a prom sendoff. He was a perfect gentleman. He was cordial to the family. When it was time to go, he opened the door for me and held my hand as we descended the stairs—a perfect gentleman.

I enjoyed the conversation of dating for several months. We would talk on the phone. He would sing to me. I admit I was enjoying and falling for the attention. However, my eyes were opened when my daddy said to me, in a conversation, "Carol, don't ever allow someone to make a fool out of you." I decided I would visit my sister for Christmas and naturally visit him as well. Boy, was I glad I did? I discovered that the relationship was not meant for me. I believed he was so involved with the dead that he couldn't appreciate the living. When sharing my thoughts with a friend, she laughed and reminded me that it's what the man does for a living. Others thought he was a good catch because of his profession.

I had to be honest with myself after enjoying the attention and ask God's will for my life. It was critical in that season because of recent losses that fleshly desires did not govern me but God's will, purpose, and plan for my life.

After experiencing recent losses, watch your new relationships. Don't be governed by the emotions of your pain and flesh that you find yourself in something further down the road you regret. Allow God to be your compass even in new relationships. I know you're tired, and during the loss, you want someone other than God to comfort you! I pray you find the strength to wait. We may not want to wait, but it will save us unnecessary pain in the future!

(Well, my niece! Auntie got the experience of being treated like a queen, even if it was only for a brief period of time. You will one day be able to look down from heaven on the day of my wedding and say, "there's my auntie!" I don't know when! I am waiting on God! God, in His timing, is going to give your aunt the desires of her heart. Auntie will always love you!)

It wasn't until I started writing this project, I realized one could experience grief related to the loss of self. Unfortunately, the loss of self can occur from an array of factors. I discovered I lost myself from early childhood due to relational issues with my mother, being molested, being bullied, and physical and emotional losses; I allowed that to define me. I adapted to who everyone wanted Carol to be or become. Not only did I adapt, but I also became who others wanted me to be or become. Little did I know this would affect me for the rest of my life. Yes, my loss of self would cause me to become stuck not only in grief but in a behavioral pattern of pleasing others over loving myself.

We can become so consumed with living our lives to please others when they are no longer in our world due to death or relationships ending that we can't function. The Lord wants us to make a fresh start and gain our self-worth back. The Lord wants us to start dethroning the people we've made gods in our world instead of allowing God to be God of our world.

I spent most of my life living in my parents' world, particularly my mother's that I feel a part of me never experienced life. As much as there was a conflict in our relationship, it was still my desire to make her happy if I could, with hopes of having a mother-daughter relationship.

We will get to a point in life where the dethroning of other gods becomes as easy as the revelation of needing help when the pain becomes real. I am reminded of a conversation with my former pastors. My father decided to start dating ten years after my mother died. I didn't accept or handle this well. I was the leader of the intercessory prayer team. I tried to cover up how I was feeling. For a season, I would assign others to pray and avoid leading prayer. I was struggling with God. I felt I couldn't pray for others while I was angry with God. My dad was the only remaining person close to me, and he was giving someone else attention.

I was in a meeting with my former pastors, and I am not even sure how we got on the subject of me not praying. They informed me they noticed that I have not been praying at the church. I am not sure if they were quite ready for my next words. I admitted I was struggling with praying because I was angry with God. I then poured out my heart concerning my dad dating. The First Lady said something profound, "Carol, all your life; you've idolized your dad to the point he actually in some cases became your god, and now the struggle is he's being removed so God can get back on the throne."

I admit I tuned the First Lady out about my dad being my god even though I knew her words were true. My relationship with my dad was one I wished my mother, and I had. My dad always told me I could be anything I wanted to be. My dad was always in my world and a part of my world. When my mother died, I felt like he was all I had, and how dare God remove the closest person to me. So, I fought the process!

My dad's dating bothered me for so many reasons. My dad was finding love again. I was over 45 years old and had been on less than five dates, had no significant other, never been married, and had no children. My dad's dating bothered me because he felt the need not be truthful with me about it. My dad had mentioned they were going away. I talked to him before leaving and asked him directly was he going to marry her. He told me no. I am not sure what happened because he informed me that he was getting married when he came home. One of the greatest things that bothered me was how much she looked like my mother, and one of her favorite fragrances is the same as my mother's.

The Lord gave me strength daily to get through such a season in my life. I never in all my years thought me and my father would ever have a strong disagreement about anything. I never thought that my father would say any hurting words to me. Well, one day we argued about him getting married. His following words pierced my heart, "Carol, the real problem is you're jealous. You're upset because you don't have anybody."

The other most significant challenge is sharing my dad with another woman other than my mother. I know this sounds selfish, and I take ownership of that. Now I understand the importance of words and how they can come back and haunt you. I always told my parents that should something happen to either of them, "I am not having a stepmother or stepfather." I recently realized that the acceptance of my stepmother has a lot to do with words I had already put into the atmosphere.

I was stuck for years in grief when my mother died. I felt myself going backward when my dad married someone who was just like my mother. The Lord had to help me and continues to help me not to regress but continue my progress.

The change in the relationship with my dad has been a challenge for me. We used to have beautiful conversations about any and everything. My dad would call and make sure I was okay. Now it's different. My dad is not the dad I have always known. Over the past few years, Father's Day has been challenging because of the relationship change and his health challenge. Yes, this is a form of grief! I had to ask the Lord to help me a week with my emotions. I had to remember that God is a good, good Father. I had to remember no matter the relationship challenges or his health challenges, the blessing is my father is still with me. I had to shift my perspective.

We often expect people who enter our lives to stay for a lifetime. Unfortunately, that's not always the case. Even when they seem like they're in our worlds for a lifetime, the season may eventually shift. As I am writing this book, I'm grieving a relationship change. I've been a faithful and consistent friend for eighteen plus years. Admittedly, the relationship may have been changing, but I wasn't aware. The person behaved in a way I felt didn't make them look good in people's sight. I thought as a friend, I should mention it. I sent a text and suggested they consider counseling. God knows my heart and intent were pure when I sent the text. They were upset, and a lengthy connection has become one of if you have a question – nothing more.

The greatest challenge during this time is knowing my assignment as an intercessor is to cover them. I've asked the Lord daily to be released from this assignment, with the answer being no. I have obeyed the Lord in completing my assignment, and thus, continue to pray for them. It's not easy praying for someone who's causing you pain! However, the Lord requires my obedience. I am getting through this daily by asking the Lord to help me with my heart and not become bitter and ease the aches of my heart. I've also asked the Lord to show the person my heart and my intentions.

I found it interesting to request a meeting with the person. The person took a month or longer to discuss what I was feeling. The person informed me of not having a problem with our friendship. They reported they didn't have a problem with my heart either but my mouth. The person struggled with me being honest with them. Based on the meeting, it was clear they were harboring lingering issues about communication. Upon leaving the meeting, it was clear despite what they said, our friendship had changed. I haven't heard from the person on a friendly level since the meeting.

I want to tell you this loss right here hurts! I never thought this friendship would come to an end! Only God knows if there will be restoration. The conflict in this relationship brings up my struggle with relationships with the fear of individuals dying or leaving. You may ask, why would I say these words. I have several incidences where this has happened. I had one year of enjoying the mother I wish I had for years. I enjoyed her company, and she even told me she loved me; and I sensed she meant it! I decided it was finally time for me to move to my place. She asked me not to leave her. I know she asked me not to leave her, but four years later, she left me. A year later, I am taking her to the doctor and getting her assessed for Alzheimer's, and three years later, she's dead. What I didn't know is that I would become her caregiver. The Lord knew if we hadn't resolved the conflict, there's no way I would've been able to take care of her. All my life my mother compared me to my older sister. I NEVER could do anything right in my mother's eyes, but my sister was the princess in my mother's world. Where was she during these three years? My sister had a tough time dealing with being a caregiver for her mother. I found this information after our mother died. I had to let my sister know how I was feeling. My sister informed me she simply couldn't do it! I am not sure what made her think that I could.

You're wondering why I'm sharing this information. I am sharing this information because I want to help someone enduring the same type of pain. You haven't shared your pain with anyone. The truth is you're done with people. You don't want to take the risk to develop friendships anymore. You're tired of loving people, and they don't love you back. The Lord sees your pain and is concerned about it. The Lord sees your tears and is concerned about them. Yes, He's an unfailing friend. I pray you to find the strength to take the risk of embracing friendships and loving again. Please don't isolate yourself! As a dear friend always advised, "Don't be bitter; God has better."

Chapter 3

Purpose of My Loss

I didn't understand the purpose of the losses in my life. I honestly wanted out of them all. It wasn't until recently that I understood their purpose. It wasn't about me! It was about what God wanted to do in me and through me. Yes, God wanted to do something in me and through me.

I know it doesn't make sense. But God wanted to uproot the things that had been holding me hostage. God wanted to uproot the co-dependent spirit. Although I thought I was an independent person, I was co-dependent on my parents and my niece. I always lived in my parents' world and found it difficult to live outside it. I was always living for my parents and never living for Carol. It wasn't until my dad got remarried that the co-dependent spirit began to break.

I was co-dependent on my father, always being consistent in my world. The reality was when the marriage took place, my dad was no longer always there. The pain of this shift! Carol had to totally rely on the Lord for complete help! I was to receive the 2021 Bold Brave & Beautiful Unbreakable Spirit Award through an organization founded by Theresa Royal Brown I wanted my dad and stepmother to be in attendance, but the price of the tickets was a detriment. My dad said, "No, we won't be attending; it's too much money." I can never recall my dad saying no to me. My stepmother sensing it was important to me told my dad, "You can go ahead and go. I don't have to." But I wanted them both to be there. The no response remained. I had to ask the Lord to help me not feel abandoned and rejected.

I was co-dependent on my niece to be the bridgetender working to repair and develop a closer relationship with my sister. The Wednesday before my niece died, I had a very heated conversation with my sister. I was not processing why she couldn't attend my graduation in Chicago. My niece and her friend were planning on attending. Moments after that conversation, my niece called me, and we talked for a long time about the argument with her mother. She shared how patience needed to be at work because her mother was getting older. She also told me when the conversation switch to my dad's upcoming wedding that she had given her mother some instructions. She told me, "I've already told my mother she needs to stay with you at the house to help you get dress. I also told her she needs to be there for you."

God used the losses to begin the process of uprooting rejection and abandonment. When you have experienced so many losses, it's easy to become friends with these two powerful sentiments. The rejection is real because you feel like no one else understands you or even wants to be around you. According to the Merriam-Webster Dictionary, the word abandoned means "left without needed protection, care, or support." The abandonment is real because you feel the person who is no longer present in your world has abandoned you. The person may no longer be physically present, but the Lord is with you protecting you, caring for you, and supporting you. He will also send individuals who can do the same. It's a matter of completely depending on Him and allowing Him to be who He is.

I had to understand with all the losses I was not rejected or abandoned. I am not abandoned because the Lord will never leave me nor forsake me. I am not only accepted in The beloved of Christ but loved and accepted by others.

The enemy wants you to think you're rejected and abandoned. You're not! The Lord loves you unconditionally and is there for you. The Lord loves you! Yes, some may not understand you. People don't realize at times; we don't even understand ourselves on this journey. The lie from the enemy is that no one understands you or loves you. Even if there's a remnant, you're loved by others. Embrace the love of remnant! Embrace the love of the remnant! Embrace the love of the remnant! I purposely typed the words three times to get it into your spirit you're loved by others. Wrap your arms around yourself and tell yourself God loves me, and others love me.

The enemy knows if he can get you to feel like God and others don't love you. The next thing that occurs is isolation. You then begin to move from isolation to depression. Even as you're reading, you may feel isolated, lonely, and hopeless. I want you to know that God is the God of hope. I decree and declare the God of hope is being released as you read these words.

The Lord is uprooting all these feelings from me. I understand isolation, loneliness, and depression. When my mother died, I isolated myself from people. I felt that no one understood my pain. I felt so lonely, and yes, depressed. I had all these symptoms until the point of not wanting to live any longer. You're going to live through the loss. Yes, you are! Live! Live!

Suicide is real! Yes, you're trying to figure out how you're going to live without your family member being present! Yes, you're trying to figure out how you're going to live without a job. Yes, you're trying to figure out how you're going to live without your body functioning like it used to. You're not going to function in your own strength. You're going to function in the strength of God! It's going to require relying totally on the Lord! It's going to require total reliance on the Lord.

If you're struggling with thoughts of suicide, please draw strength from the Lord but reach out for help. There is help available for you! You can call the National Suicide Prevention Lifeline at 1-800-273-8255. Perhaps someone has confided in you about feeling suicidal. Reach out for help on their behalf. You can call the police or take them to the hospital if you're able to get them to go with you.

The Lord is using loss to teach me to relinquish my control. I admit having to ask the Lord to help me with control. I've recently looked by over my life and discovered the control challenges stem from being the only child raised in our family home and honestly always getting what I wanted. I've always been told by friends that I am spoiled. And they are right, my parents spoiled me.

Parents, spoiling your children may have negative consequences in your children's lives that may linger into adulthood. It's important to consistently inform your children, although I am giving you everything you want, the real world and even God are not going to always going to do the same. It will help them live. It was one of my biggest challenges; and I am still learning the lessons of the challenge.

God and I have had several conversations concerning the losses in my life. I remember at one point hearing, "Carol, I am not going to give you everything you want even if you throw a tantrum. I am God, and I am in control, not you!" I admit I was upset with hearing God tell me these words. However, I realized that no matter how I tried to control the outcome of the loss experience, I had to submit it all to God and allow Him to be in complete control.

My being in control caused me years of being stuck in grief and bondage. I was determined to do things my way. I was determined to keep attending church but not serving, not praying consistently and not studying my word privately. I had totally disconnected from The Vine, the real source of my strength. I began to live a life of hopelessness and defeat because I was unplugged. The reason why I couldn't maneuver through the dark tunnel of grief is that I was disconnected from of the Source of my light.

Plug back into your source. You're reading these words, and you've unplugged from your source. The Lord is calling you back to Him. You're trying to manage something in your strength that's too much. I always tell my support group, "Strength for the Grieving by the Grieving," the same thing I've said multiple times in this book, don't try to do grief without God. Yes, even during all your losses and emotions, don't do grief without God. Include God in every aspect of your world, including the losses.

I heard Pastor Steven Furtick, Elevation Church, say, "Instead of asking God why did this happen? We should ask God, 'What are you doing in my life?' And not how long are you going to leave me here?" I never thought to ask God the purpose of loss. The purpose of loss started manifesting when my mother died. I didn't want anyone to go through the pain I experienced alone. I wanted to help other grieving individuals.

I became too excited to help others and shared my vision with the wrong person. Be careful in sharing your vision. Everyone is not in support of your vision, even if you think they are. Everyone is not for you or in your corner. I informed my former pastor of my vision. His response was disheartening, "Carol, no one is going to want to participate because it's too morbid."

I allowed his words to stop me from pursuing what God had given me. However, when your vision is God ordained it will come to pass. December 2016 I was scrolling through Facebook and saw a post from my friend Carol Alsbrooks. She was encouraging people to check on those in a season of loss, after the funeral and when everyone is going on about their business. Upon reading her post, I felt a leap in my stomach. The vision was coming alive.

As a result of Carol's post, I was unable to sleep that night. I tossed and turned all night. I awakened at six A.M. with the Lord giving specific instructions. "Get up and start a Facebook group for grieving individuals." I replied with a question, "Lord, what am I going to name the group?" The Lord replied, "Strength for the Grieving by the Grieving." I got up and created the group.

Carol Alsbrooks was the first member to join and then she started inviting others to join. The group started growing the first day. As of July 1, 2021, we have more than 300 members. To God Be All the Glory!

Strength for the Grieving was birthed out of my pain and God's purpose in me to see others supported through a difficult journey. We will turn five years old in December 2021. The Lord is faithful!

Our purpose for our losses is not about us! We don't do it intentionally, yet at times we do make it all about us. We often have series of questions: Why don't they see my pain? Why aren't people here? We miss the bigger picture. Please know as I write these words, I am asking myself: How many years did I miss the bigger picture? How many people remained stuck, depressed, or even ended their lives because I was self-centered in my pain instead of being God-centered? Let's pause and tell ourselves we will no longer be self-centered, but God-centered.

Jesus loves us so much! We were the purpose for Jesus' pain. We're the product of Jesus enduring the pain. Who is the purpose of your pain? What is the product of your pain? I had no idea the pain of loss I endured would later prove helpful for a group of individuals, although our journeys are different, we have pain as a common denominator. The purpose of my pain was to produce a tool the Lord uses to produce productivity in the lives of members of the group.

People don't talk about suicide or share their stories. Suicide is real. I struggled with it. My suicidal thoughts started early. The root of my suicidal thoughts - rejection and word curses. As a child being bullied and always the last person to get picked for teams. I was the left-over person. They didn't want me on their team, but Jesus thought I was worthy to be a part of His. He accepted me in The beloved. I had to learn to reject the language of suicide whenever it came to my mind. I had to start replacing the word curses from others with God's Word concerning my identity.

Someone reading can honestly relate to being called everything but a Child of God. You've masked all the thoughts and emotions to please others. You're silently struggling with thoughts of suicide. You've had enough! You feel like you've lost the fight! You want out of what you feel like is hell. I've come to speak to your spirit and soul, and command you to live. God loves you, and your life matters to Him and me. My brothers and sisters, you are fearfully and wonderfully made. God thought enough of you to create you! Yes, people may have called you out of your name. God calls you by your name! He loves you so much; He allowed you the ability to read these words and give you another chance to live life. You can live and live life to the fullest. You will live and live life to the fullest. The devil has lost the battle! Yes, he has!

I mentioned earlier I was always taught if you kill yourself, you're going to hell. But I never thought about going to hell when the suicidal thoughts entered my mind. I always thought what I was experiencing was hell on Earth, and I wanted out. I am not blaming my mother. I look back and think maybe she didn't know to get me professional help. The other side is I am not sure if my mother believed in professional help. I strongly believe my mother felt God could fix everything. I do believe that He can, but also believe we must collaborate with God in some areas of our lives for our complete healing. Faith without works is dead. Yes, we can believe God for our mental healing. The work comes to play by getting professional help when needed. Getting professional help doesn't change your relationship with God. I pray in this season, as more people are struggling with their mental health, we stop automatically sending them to hell. Pray for the person and then help them get the professional help needed.

The Lord will give you beauty for ashes! The Lord will allow you to experience joy in losses. I honestly never thought I would say, "I am glad to be alive." I told the Lord at the beginning of 2021, with tears streaming down my face, "Lord, thank You that I am alive." I meant those words. I am grateful to be alive. The Lord kept me alive not only to be a blessing to others but so I could see the goodness of the Lord in my land! Yes, you are going to live to see the goodness of the Lord in the land of the living. Don't you give up now! You've come to close.

God's promises over my life were present while I was trying to end it. God kept me alive to see the manifestation of His promises concerning my life. God kept you alive to see the manifestation of promises concerning your life. The promises of God will be fulfilled in your life! Yes, tell yourself, "The promises of God will be fulfilled in my life!"

Our purpose is not predicated on what people say we are. Our purpose is predicated on what God says we are. It's hard at times to believe God has a purpose and plan for our lives when all we've heard is we will never amount to anything.

I was tending to my own business one day and heard the Lord say, "Carol, you are somebody." I said, "Thank You, Lord." He continued to speak, "Carol, start writing an e-devotional entitled, *You Are Somebody Seed of the Month*. I obeyed the Lord when I heard Him in 2004, and I continue to write that monthly e-devotional.

The Lord continued to provide me with instructions. The next instruction was to start a radio broadcast entitled, "You Are Somebody!" The Lord gave me favor to host "You Are Somebody Radio Broadcast" on WFAX 1220 AM in Falls Church, Virginia for four and a half years. I didn't know what the Lord was doing. I simply obeyed. When others think we're nobody, God views us differently. God knows the thoughts and plans for our lives. Thoughts of good and not evil to give us an expected end. (Jeremiah 29:11) God is giving you and me an expected end even the midst of loss and pain, and it is great! Great Pain, Great Gain!

How do you know your purpose despite all your loss? You may try to abort your purpose, but loss doesn't abort the purpose of God on your life unless you allow it. Here are questions that may help you discover your purpose: What's your passion? As a child, what did you always want to be when you became an adult? What would you do for free without any problems? What causes a strong burden in your spirit? What solutions do you have to someone else's problems? What negative experience did you survive?

When I was a child, I loved to teach my babysitter's son. My babysitter would say, "Carol, you will make a great teacher one day!" I enjoyed playing school as a child and being the teacher. I also enjoyed pretending to be a nurse as a child. I had a play stethoscope; I would place it on my friends' chests. I didn't know what I was expecting to hear. Who knew the interest as a child would become my purpose as an adult?

I attended Crossland Vocational School in my last year of high school. I was in the nursing assistant program. I became a Certified Nursing Assistant (CNA) and started working two weeks after graduation at Sibley Memorial Hospital. I worked as a nursing assistant putting myself through nursing school. Nursing school was no joke! I became a Registered Nurse in 1997. I've been in health care for 32 years and have been honored to care for countless individuals and families.

I remember receiving my Ministerial Licenses and being upset with God about doors opening for other individuals but not for me. I was in the bathroom one morning, and the Lord said, "Carol, the doors aren't opening because you're not called to preach but teach. If you submit to your calling, you will see doors opening." I admit I didn't want to be a teacher of God's Word. I thought teachers were boring. I also thought people's response to teachers was dull. I wanted to see people yell, clap, and scream when I spoke. It's my truth! I realized that was all Carol and not God.

Once I gave God a yes to what He called and anointed me to do, doors began to open. The doors were not in the pulpit, but they still were doors. Often clergy miss doors because they're waiting on the pulpit. The teaching door of being the Director of Education for the HIV/AIDS Ministry was great. Teaching was my passion, and I excelled as the instructor for the HIV 101 class. I also had the wonderful opportunity to be the Instructor for Phase III HIV/AIDS education at Calvary's Alternative to Alcohol and Drug Abuse House. I was featured in the Washington Times while presenting at the Boys and Girls Club in Washington DC. I was honored to be asked to go to Uganda in 2010 and teach women about HIV/AIDS. These doors occurred from a sincere yes to God's purpose and plan for my life.

As I was writing concerning purpose, I recalled a loss that was attached to purpose. I lost a dear friend to HIV/AIDS. I started noticing she was losing a large amount of weight. I also noticed the coloration of her skin. I surmised that she had HIV/AIDS. I later discovered my thoughts were correct. I further found out she didn't want me to know this information for fear I would no longer want to be her friend or come around her.

God clearly placed me in my friend's life for a purpose. Unfortunately, she faced the real stigma associated with HIV/AIDS. I was working as a nursing assistant when she was admitted to a local hospital. I received a call from her saying the care she was receiving was terrible. The staff would not help her with her hygiene. I would leave work sometimes, go to the hospital, and do what medical professionals should have been doing. Her family had a birthday party for her while she was in the hospital. As I wheeled her to the room where the party was being held, one family member said, "thank you so much for wheeling her." There was a dismissive look on the family's face. I said, "You're welcome; I am not her nurse but one of her friends." The family member apologized, "I thought you were one of the nurses."

My friend was discharged from the hospital to return home to an environment where the stigma continued. Her family was struggling with taking care of her at home, so I went to the house and did it. I paid a price for this with my mother particularly. My mother treated me as if I was infected with HIV/AIDS, and she would catch it from me.

I received the stigma of HIV/AIDS from my mother without being infected. My mother would bleach all the plates and utensils. I remember leaving a can of soda on the counter. My niece saw the can, picked it up to start drinking. My mother yelled, "Wait Theresa! Put that can down! You don't want to drink behind Carol. She's taking care of a lady that has HIV/AIDS." I was not too fond of the treatment as if I was contagious in my own home. My heart began to feel heavy for my friend and anyone infected with HIV/AIDS.

My friend eventually went home to be with the Lord. I still remember the events of her death like it was yesterday. I was at work, and she happened to cross my mind. I called one of her dearest friends to see how she was doing. That friend was actually at her bedside and told me she wasn't doing well. I went straight to the hospital after getting off work. Upon arriving in the room, I looked at my friend and sensed her transition was closer than I thought. I began to pray and ask the Lord to allow her transition before visiting hours were over. I stood at the side, holding her hand. I watched her breathing become labored. I noticed her breathing become slower. I looked at the clock, and it was getting closer to visiting hours being over (8:00 P.M.). I squeezed her hand at eight, she gasped and then there was no more breathing. She was gone. I laid my head briefly on her chest

The day of her funeral was difficult for so many reasons. I had to deal with my own emotions. I had to push aside my emotions toward individuals who would get up and start sharing their words of expressions concerning her. I wondered where they were during the last months and weeks of her life. Where were they when she needed them the most?

When the family saw me walking in the church, they allowed me to sit in the section with them. They gave me an envelope, and with tears in their eyes. I opened the envelope when I got home, but the words I will never forget from them impacted me. "Thank you, Carol, for doing what we never could've done."

My friend's death caused me to want to do something in her honor. I decided to apply for a nursing position at Whitman Walker Clinic in Washington, DC. Whitman Walker was instrumental in her HIV/AIDS care. Whitman Walker offered me the job. The

Director of Nursing informed me others were more qualified than me, but he felt that I was a caring soul. I was the day treatment nurse in the morning and worked in the clinic in the afternoon.

I loved working at Whitman Walker. I learned a lot from my patients and I believe I made an impact in their lives. I remember walking down the street one day, and one of my patients saw me. They ran up to me and gave me a big hug. When I received my Ministerial License, one of my patients was determined to come and support me. The Day Treatment Program offered Bible study as part of their program. There was a pastor who was very instrumental in the patient spiritual care. She would come and teach Bible study every week. When she couldn't teach, the Director of the Program asked me to do it. I was honored and the patients were very receptive.

I was also responsible for teaching a Medication Management Adherence class weekly. It's where we talked about their medications and how they were doing taking them. I had an idea one day while teaching the group to start a reading group. I asked the director if I could start the group, and without hesitation, he agreed. I knew reading was a challenge for some in the group. I decided the book of choice would be the *Purpose Driven Life* by Rick Warren. We would listen to a section of the book each week. My clients appreciated me taking care of them while being compassionate. My experience of my mother's stigma toward me even without being infected and my friend's death caused me to make sure I showed compassion to each patient.

I had no idea me honoring my friend by working at Whitman Walker would start opening doors. I remember Dormetria Robinson Thompson called looking for someone to teach the youth at her church about HIV/AIDS. They referred Dormetria to me. I accepted the invitation; taught the sessions, and she and I ended becoming friends. I even caught her bouquet at her wedding. I often laugh at the myth that the person who catches the bouquet is next to get married. Her bouquet was the second one I'd caught. I am just as single as the day I came out of my mother's womb.

We often negatively view loss. However, at times even in loss, positive things happen. It's all about our perspective.

Chapter 4

Perspective in the Midst of Loss

How do you view your loss? What comes to your mind when you think of your loss? If you're like me, the first thought that comes to mind is I'm not going to make it through this. The second thought that comes to mind is, "How am I going to make it through this? The last thought that comes to mind is that I don't know how I will live without the loss.

I always viewed my loss as the end of my world. I realized I negatively shaped my world for years around an errant perspective on the losses in my world. Let's define perspective before we continue. According to Merriam-Webster's Dictionary, perspective is defined as the "capacity to view things in their true relations or relative of importance."

My perspective on loss was that my life would never be the same and I couldn't live without the thing or person that was lost. I felt this when my niece died. My niece was my biggest cheerleader and support system. She would encourage me and be present. I never had to wonder or second, guess her presence. When you rely on others to encourage you and cheer you on to victory, what do you do when they're no longer around? You become your own cheerleader. The struggle with becoming our own cheerleader is not seeing and appreciating the value of our worth. Yes, other people see the greatness in us. However, do we know the greatness in ourselves? It has taken me years to see the greatness inside of me and the value I bring to the lives of others. Yes, my brothers and my sisters, you're valuable to God and others. The key is to believe it and believe in yourself. Place your hands on your chest and repeat, "I believe in me!"

I want you to remember the Lord believes in you and trusts you with whatever gifts and talents He's given you. Now that you believe in yourself, trust God in you and yourself. I am not sure who needs to read these words. You're not your past. Your present and future are bright. You're no longer bound by your past, and the word curses spoken over you! You, my brothers, and sisters, are free to be! Yes, place your hand on your chest again and say, "I am free to be!"

We can shift our perspective by understanding our lives matter! Our lives matter to God and others. I may not know you, but your life matters to me.

Our perspective has everything to do with mindset. What are we thinking? We can change our actions by changing our thoughts. What are you thinking? The Bible says in *Philippians 4:8 (KJV)* – *"Finally brethren whatsoever things are true, whatsoever things are just, whatsoever things are pure, whatsoever things are lovely, whatsoever things are of good report, if there be any praise think on these things."* We often allow our thoughts to dwell on the negative aspects of loss. I know I did. I never thought to dwell on things true. The truth is I can make it despite the losses. The truth is I can live despite the losses. As it relates to the death of a loved one, please know making it and learning to live without them IS NOT me telling anyone to get over the death of a loved one. I want you to know there's life after loss!

The enemy wants us to stay focused on the lies; so, he keeps whispering in our ears the lies he knows we will believe. He knows that if we ever grab hold of truth and consistently rehearse truth and not the lies, we will be free and stay free.

Individuals don't think of health issues as concerns related to loss. Well, health issues can be a form of loss. This loss is when you're no longer able to do things the way you use to do them. An example is walking with a limp or with the aid of a crutch, cane, or walker. Perhaps you received the report that you would never walk again without devices or a limp. You can choose to believe the report or choose to believe the report of God. With God all things are possible!

I was informed years ago I would never be able to walk without a cane or walker. I had a bad fall that required reconstruction of my left ankle. I have plates on both sides and pins in that ankle. I was also told never to fall again. Unfortunately, I have had several falls since that warning. I never dwelt on the report that I would never walk again. I dwelt on the God who I know as a healer. I am walking without any aid of devices.

I am currently walking with a limp. Over the past two years, I've been in pain without the doctors knowing the cause of pain and how to treat it. I've spent money on doctor visits, weeks in physical therapy, and medications, all without any resolution.

My primary care physician referred me to a rheumatologist. The rheumatologist, after examination, told me the source of my pain before x-rays. He took x-rays and says," I hate to tell you this news, but you have severe arthritis in your hip, and surgery is needed." The orthopedic doctor forewarned me of arthritis but never mentioned it would be severe and said surgery was the last choice. I was numbed by the rheumatologist's report.

That report brought up one of my worst fears. Who is going to take care of me when I become sick? How am I going to deal with being cared for after surgery? The fear of being sick with no one to take care of me is real. I live alone with no children, and my dad is elderly. The Lord quickly reminded me I believed a lie. He reminded me to remember four years ago when I had a rotator cuff repair on my dominant shoulder. I never wanted or lacked care. He sent me caregivers and everything I needed.

I had started to dwell on these thoughts. I quickly took a deep breath and went into the presence of the Lord. I addressed my fears to the Lord and called Him who He is. I asked the Lord for direction and guidance for the next phase of my healing. The Lord quickly reminded me of who He was and to wait on His timing. I am trusting and believing in God! I walk every day and say, "I am not going to always walk with a limp. I am healed." I am anointing my leg and hip with oil and plead the Blood of Jesus! I grabbed whole of my downcast thoughts.

Hold on to your faith regardless of the negative doctor's report and think on the good report found in God's Word. The devil wants to make us think God doesn't see or hear our pleas for help. The devil is a liar and the father of all lies. I pray in this season you will become familiar with the good report of God's Word.

I didn't believe I could make it without loss or serve in ministry. When my mother died, I shut completely down. I stopped serving in ministry. It's important to take a break and be okay with allowing yourself to grieve. Be careful of that break turning into an extended vacation. I had become comfortable waddling in a place where God hadn't prepared for me. God had already prepared joy and rest. I was too blinded by emotions to embrace and experience it.

I decree and declare even as you're reading these words, you're going to find joy and rest in His presence. I know you want the presence of others. Other individuals, however, can't supply the joy and rest as the Lord can. It's in His presence we experience the fullness of joy at His right-hand are pleasures forevermore. See, the joy you will experience is everlasting because of who God is. God is an everlasting Father!

Mothers' Day 2021 was my first time serving in a ministry capacity at church. I ended up filling in for the Elder scheduled to pray. I heard the Lord give me instructions to encourage someone about how the special day was a challenge and shared my testimony of it being my first Mothers' Day completing a ministry assignment since my mother died.

I had to change my perspective to stand in prayer. I told myself I would be okay to feel what I feel. I also told myself I was going to experience joy and not stay in a place of sadness. I was determined to be happy. I got through it relying on the Lord's strength. I realized I didn't have to be strong; the Lord is my strength in weakness. I celebrated my accomplishments. My ability to pray publicly that day may not have been major to anyone else, but it was to me. I now understand the importance of giving myself grace.

Give yourself grace during loss. Yes, give yourself the grace to make mistakes and not be perfect. Forgive yourself. Giving yourself grace plays a significant role in your perspective.

I was flipping through the Netflix movie section and saw a movie entitled *Greater*. I didn't pay any further attention to it, in fact, I logged off Netflix and turned-on CNN. The next day I heard the Lord instruct me to watch *Greater*.

The movie is based on the true story of Brandon Burlsworth, who experiences the loss of identity due to being bullied, loss of relationship with his father, death of a father, and loss of numerous football games, including the championship. Despite the experience of multiple losses, he kept moving and become productive. The unique part is his movement and productivity amid loss left a legacy for future generations.

A change of perspective can not only allow movement and productivity but leave a legacy. The University of Arkansas gives eighteen scholarships each year in honor of Brandon Burlsworth. The Brandon Burlsworth Foundation gives free eye care to thousands of underprivileged children. The Burls Kids gives free tickets to each Razorback and Colts home game. Marty, Brandon's surviving brother leads the Brandon Burlsworth Football Camp. The camp teaches faith in God, the importance of family and academics, and of course - football.

Brandon, although faced with much loss, allowed God to be God! He was able to see who God is during every loss!

Chapter 5

Who is God in the Midst of Loss?

I know many of us may not want to ask the question who God is during loss. We may prefer to ask where is God in the midst of loss? God is God – even during loss. Loss gives us the ability to see the characteristics of God manifested. The enemy will try and use loss to distract us from seeing God in the midst of loss.

When the incident happened with the ceiling falling, I had no idea how any of it was going to come together. I wasn't worried because I had more confidence in God than the landlord because of history and experience. That history ignited my faith and confidence in God to perform what He said He would.

My last bout with loss pulled me into recalling my history and experiences with God. While focused on those things, I further increased my faith and confidence in God. In the situation with the roof, my confidence was not in the landlord or what the legal system could force in vindication. anyone else. I had to not think anything in my world was strange, but that it was for a purpose. It was quite uncomfortable to lean into that perspective because I was not use to it, but loss had pushed me into peace.

When my mother died, I felt I was in a place of being alone. I viewed everyone else having someone to be their support. Was this the truth or my false reality? Didn't I have God? Did I have them (whoever I was viewing) as my support and others?

God never left me nor forsook me, why, because I am part of God's DNA. God is part of my DNA. God can't leave who He's intertwined with. God was always with me because I am apart of Him. During loss, the focus often shifts to a physical touch instead of a God touch. When this happens, the void stays for years. God is trying to push through so much to get to us. God is in the background screaming; "I am here!" "I am Jehovah Azar!" (The Lord my help) "I am Jehovah Nissi!" (The Lord my banner). "I am Jehovah Rapha!" (The Lord that heals). "But I'll wait my turn because I am a gentleman."

The losses I experienced caused me to feel like I was walking in a dark tunnel. Once I plugged back into The Light, which is God I was able to see in the tunnel and see light at the end of the tunnel. I was able to see because Jesus is The Light of the world, including mine. He is the best illuminator. The Bible reads in *Psalm 18:28 KJV*- *"For thou wilt light my candle: the LORD my God will enlighten my darkness."*

You may feel like you're in a dark tunnel too and unable to see your way through. If you have unplugged from your source of light, plug back in. If you haven't unplugged, remember you have light built inside of you. I decree and declare, LIGHT BE ACTIVATED!

The Lord is our Rock during loss. *Psalm 61:2 KJV* reads, *"from the end of the Earth will I cry unto thee, when my heart is overwhelmed: lead me to the Rock that is higher than I."* I was at the grave of my mother one day and noticed a rock. I wasn't sure why it caught my attention. I heard the Lord say, "Carol, stand on the rock." Well, I am a full-figured girl, I don't like to sit on anything that I feel is not going to support me, let alone stand on something like a rock. I was concerned the rock would sink into the ground based on my weight. I obeyed God and stood on it. As I stepped off the rock, I looked down and saw that it was in the same exact location. The rock hadn't sunk into the ground. I then heard the Lord say, "I am going to be your rock during your loss. I will be able to carry your weight." It gave so much powerful meaning to the lyrics to that old hymnal, "…on Christ the Solid Rock I stand, all other ground is sinking sand." And then I hear the lyrics by gospel singer Dottie Rambo, "Where do I go when there's nobody else to turn to? Who am I gonna talk to when nobody wants to listen? Who do I lean on when there's no foundation stable? I go to The Rock. I know He's able. I go to The Rock." Yes, The Rock, God, The Father can hold us up!

My Co-Pastor, LaQuisha Brown of the House of Healing DMV, preached one Sunday and introduced us to a name of God Jehovah Amad (The God of Supernatural Interruption). She told us to go home and place the words over the doorpost of our home. I obeyed. November 9, 2020, after the ceiling collapsed, as I was coming out of the room, I looked up and saw "Jehovah Amad", the God of Supernatural Interruption, on the doorpost. I watched God supernaturally interrupt what could've been death. God did it! We never know what our obedience to our leaders can bring, even when we may not understand it. I am so glad I obeyed God.

In the loss, the Lord is our shield, our glory, and the lifter up of our heads. (Psalm 3:3) Yes, we're shielded from all attacks of the enemy during loss. The Lord knows at times loss will cause us to have our heads down with tears streaming down our face, but He can dry all our tears, and console us like no one else. *"Lift our heads, oh ye gates, and be ye lift up ye everlasting doors; and the King of glory shall come in. Who is this King of glory? The Lord strong and mighty, the Lord might in battle."* (Psalm 24:7-10)

In the loss, we have Jehovah-Gibbor Milchamah (the Lord mighty in battle). Yes, the Lord is with us, fighting for us when we can't fight. The good part is He's never lost a battle. Allow Him to fight, and rest in Him while He does! The battle isn't ours but the Lord!

The Lord is our provider. You're His seed and His responsibility. David says it best, *"I've been young, and now am old; yet have I not seen the righteous forsaken, nor his seed begging bread."* Psalm 37:25 (KJV) I know it may seem like lack; however, it's not about what we see but who we know and what we know. God will always *"supply all our needs according to His riches in glory by Christ Jesus."* (Philippians 4:19 KJV) God is going to take care of you! Yes, He is!

The Lord is faithful in midst of loss. We can't base God's faithfulness toward us on the unfaithfulness of people in our lives. God is consistent in all His attributes. *"Forever, O LORD, thy word is settled in heaven. Thy faithfulness is unto all generations: Thou hast established the Earth and it abideth."* (Psalm 119: 89-90, KJV) Let's rest in the faithfulness of God, knowing He's faithful to fulfill every promise spoken over our lives.

Chapter 6

Speaking in the Midst of Loss

What we say is important! We have the power of life and death in our mouths. As I look back over my losses, I realized had I not opened my mouth and spoke God's Word; I would've been stuck. Speaking God's Word during loss also requires belief in what we say. We only need mustard seed size faith, and we can speak to the mountain and tell it to be moved.

Let's begin to open our mouths and speak things into existence. Perhaps you don't know what to say or where to begin. I pray this chapter helps you with your confessions.

- I believe in Me!
- I got victory OVER ME!
- There's nothing God can't handle today!
- Father, I allow You to fill the void with Yourself!
- God is bringing completion to some things in my life!
- Purpose is being birthed out of my pain!
- God is greater than the pain!
- There's a shift coming to my world! I receive and walk in the shift!

- I decree and declare; I am at peace!
- God has this and me!
- Father, I choose to worship You in my place of pain!
- I am being sustained!
- Favor is on my life for the rest of my life!
- The Lord has freed me from my past!
- God always protects me!
- I will live in peace!
- The God of love and peace is with me!
- My treasure is the fear of the Lord!
- I am called to endure this hard place!
- God is the God of my struggle!
- God is God in the hard place!
- I am walking in my complete deliverance!
- I am going to conqueror the inner me and win!
- God's mindset will become my motivation!
- I will no longer be governed by my inner me!
- I identify with who God says I am!
- My fears are being released through my tears!
- My faith is about to unlock doors!
- God has preserved me!
- I know my worth!
- The residue of my life won't take me out!
- The Lord freed me from ALL my fears!
- God is holding me up!
- Wherever I go. God is with me!
- I am content in my place of loneliness!
- I will allow You to be God in every area of my life!
- I will live in today and not tomorrow!

- Lord, breathe on me again!
- I have the grace to run this race!
- The pity party is canceled! I've started a praise party!
- My faith is activated to believe God again!
- The devil doesn't have any part of my mind! My complete mind belongs to God!
- I will not break under this pressure! I will experience greatness despite it!
- I have God's strength on this emotional roller coaster!
- I survived my past! I will survive my present!
- God, I am focused on You!
- Lord, I embrace your presence!
- God has given me power to get through THIS!
- I am not drowning! I am being led to dry land!
- Walls come down!
- The Lord is rescuing me!
- I believe God for MYSELF!
- I lay aside every weight and REST!
- God is keeping me on my feet!
- I may have made mistakes, but I am not a mistake!
- My mindset has shifted!
- I will experience God's joy during this season even as my emotions unravel!
- I will magnify the promises of God and not my problems!
- I will soar above what's trying to hold me down!
- I am in my right mind, which demands a praise!
- Self, you're going to make it!
- I will stand even when it feels like I've been knocked down!

- I am hurting and crying, but I will live!
- I prepare my mind for my resurrection! Something is about to be resurrected in my life!
- Grief doesn't change the promises of God concerning my life!
- God, You promised, and I believe You!
- I pray, praise, and press through the pain!
- I won't quit or die in an uncomfortable place!
- There's nothing God can't handle!
- I am experiencing restoration and rejuvenation!
- God, You're the God of my hidden tears!
- The peace of God is released in chaos!
- There's a release of more than the devil's roar!
- I will embrace the new things in my life!
- Purpose is being birthed out my pain!
- I will not self-destruct in this season!
- Good, Good Father, continue to manifest Yourself in my world!
- The Lord will make a way as I live in today!
- I receive and walk in the shift that's coming to my world!
- Grief WILL NOT take me out!
- I am becoming someone's miracle even amid loss!
- I will be still and allow God to be God!
- Heal me God, even the areas I've had on reserve!
- I raise my praise as You raise me up!
- The furnace is hot, but I am not being burned!
- God, as You know what's best for me, I rest in You!
- I free myself from my own prison with my praise!
- I am not guilty!

- As God has forgiven me, I forgive me!
- I love ALL aspects of me!
- I am not abandoned nor neglected! I am accepted in The beloved of God!
- I speak peace to the storms of my life! Peace be still!
- I will conqueror me!
- I will see and experience goodness in my land!
- I press through stress, understanding this is only a test!
- I will take part in my own healing and deliverance!
- God, You reign over the pain!
- I am NEVER without hope! The God of hope is with me!
- I am NEVER without comfort! I have God of comfort!
- God, You're my great inheritance!
- I can see in the dark tunnel with You, God as my light!
- I no longer wait on others affirmation! You God have affirmed me!
- I am secure in You God and myself!
- God, You're my expectation!
- I will experience rebuilding, recovery, and restoration on the other side of loss.
- I release others who have hurt me!
- Great gain is coming out of this pain!
- God, You're my confidence! My confidence is in You!
- I've sown in tears, and now is my reaping season of joy!
- I am not always going to be sad!
- I rely on the Lord's strength to embrace my process and not avoid the process!
- I lay aside the weight and REST!

- God arise and let the inner me that's trying to destroy me be scattered!
- Lord, head lifter, rise in my life!
- The Lord is causing a river in my desert!
- No more procrastination related to the release of my assignment in the Earth!
- I am coming out of the grave and the grave clothes that have kept me bound!
- I rely on the strength of the Lord to embrace the uncomfortable changes in my individual world!

Chapter 7

Promises in the Midst of Loss

God is not like a man. Men will make you promises and break them. God keeps his promises! *"God is not a man, that he should lie; neither the son of man, that he should repent: hath he said, and shall he not do it? or hath he spoken, and shall he not make it good?"* (Numbers 23:19, KJV)

You may be struggling with God and with believing He will fulfill any promises during this time. God understands your struggle with Him and still loves you. Tell Him your struggle and allow Him to be the God of your struggle.

God has not changed His mind or thoughts concerning you because you're struggling with Him. He still knows the thoughts He has toward you, thoughts of peace and not evil, to give you an expected end. *(Jeremiah 29:11, KJV)* Your expected end is going to be great in the midst of loss.

I know and understand that people have made promises and haven't fulfilled them. They told you they would be with you through your journey, and three weeks after the loss, you were unable to find them. God hasn't left you! God HAS NOT LEFT YOU! God promised He would never forsake you.

Deuteronomy 31:6, KJV - "Be strong and of a good courage, fear not, nor be afraid of them: for the Lord thy God, he it is that doth go with thee; he will not fail thee, nor forsake thee." As we look at this passage of scripture, we see several promises. The first promise we see is that God goes with us! Immanuel, God with us! The following promise we see in Deuteronomy 31:6 is God will not fail us! It may feel like God has failed you, but He has not; and I know you have questions that prove you believe otherwise. Here is why I am certain:

John 14:12- "Verily, Verily, I say unto you, He that believeth on me, the works that I do shall he do also; and greater works than these shall he do."

Jeremiah 30:17- "For I will restore health unto thee, and I will heal the of thy wounds, saith the LORD; because they called thee an Outcast, saying, This is Zion, whom no man seeketh after."

Romans 8:28- "And we know that all things work together for good to them that love God, to them who are called according to his purpose. It's All working together for your good! Yes, the loss is working for your good!"

Romans 8:37- "Nay, in all these things we're more than conquerors through him that loved us! You're not just a conqueror. You're more than a conqueror. Grief will not conqueror you! You will conqueror grief!"

Psalm 30:5- "For his anger endureth but a moment, and in His favor is life; weeping may endure for a night, but joy cometh in the morning."

Psalm 30:11- "*Thou hast turned my mourning into dancing; Thou hast put off my sackcloth and girded me with gladness.*"

Psalm 55:22- "*Cast thy burden upon the Lord, and he shall sustain thee: He shall never suffer the righteous to be moved.*"

Chapter 8

Prayers in the Midst of Loss

It's not easy praying at times in the midst of loss. There are times where we don't know what to say. Honestly, we don't even want to articulate the things we are feeling, including our anger or disappointment with and in God. We struggle to find the words.

Prayer is not deep as we as Christians make it. Prayer is simply having a conversation with God. Prayer is a conversation between two individuals, not just one person. Prayer is talking to God and allowing Him to talk back. I hope we get to the point where we stop hanging up on God in the middle or the start of His conversation with us. I hope we settle ourselves after our side of the conversation with God. God does speak. Do we sit still after our conversation to listen, or do we just quickly get up? How would we feel if someone is doing all the talking, and as soon as we open our mouths to speak, we hear the dial tone? I know I wouldn't feel good at all. Do you see how much the Lord loves us? Even when we're rude to Him, doing all the talking, and not allowing Him to speak to us, He still allows us to come again and have another conversation. He even goes further, and answers requests made during our conversations.

Prayers doesn't have to be a lot of words. "Lord help" is a prayer! Whatever you say, find the strength to pray during your loss. Here are starter prayers for you! The Lord wants to hear from you in the midst of your loss. He wants to release strategies to help you in the midst of loss. As you pray these words, sit still after you speak, and listen to what He wants to say.

We cancel the lie of the devil who is telling you God doesn't hear your prayers or answer your prayers. You may not get everything you ask for, especially if it's not lining up to His will, purpose, and plan for your life. The Bible reads in *Isaiah 65:24- "And it shall come to pass, that before I call, I will answer, and while they are yet speaking, I will hear." First John 5:14- "And this is the confidence that we have in him, that if we ask anything according to his will, he heareth us."*

As you pray the will of God and listen to Him, expect Him to answer your prayers. I Don't waver in your faith while waiting.

Pain

Father, I bless and honor Your name! There's no one greater than You! I come to You being honest concerning the pain I am feeling. It hurts. I am tired of feeling this pain! It often appears each day and it is getting worst. I don't know exactly what to do. Now that I am transparent, I feel You, Lord, are another source of my pain. I believed You to turn things around in my world and not take away things. I have so many questions for You! I often hear, You're a sovereign God! My truth is I am not in the place of accepting Your sovereignty. I do ask for Your strength to help me get to this place. I also ask You to help me with my anger toward

You! I don't want to stay in this place any longer. I honestly don't know how to move from this place. I ask You to help me!

Father, I want to get to the place to allow You to reign in the midst of my pain. Please forgive me for allowing grief to reign and not allowing You to reign. I apologize! I want You to reign in the midst of my life. I dethrone everything anti-God and place You back on the throne!

I recognize even in the midst of the pain, God, You've been good. Even in the midst of my anger and frustration with You! You God kept me alive and kept my mind intact! There were days where I thought I was going to lose my mind! You kept me! Yes, in the midst of the pain, when I wanted to be held, and there was no one around, You held me close, and You are still holding me. Thank you, Lord, for holding me!

There are times where I feel like I've created floods and need Noah's Ark. However, my tears are okay with You! You understand my tears and have placed my tears in a bottle. You've even told me in Your Word weeping may endure for a night, but joy comes in the morning. Yes, I've sown in tears, now help me get to the place where I reap in joy. Thank you, kind Father, for seeing and understanding my tears!

Father, as I endure the place of pain I don't like until You decide to decrease the pain, I thank you in advance for the great gain that's coming out of this place. I do believe Your Word that the God of all "grace *who hath called us unto his eternal glory by Christ Jesus after that, ye have suffered a while, make you perfect, stablish, strengthen, settle you.*" (1 Peter 5:10, KJV). "*For I reckon that the sufferings of this present time are not worthy to be compared with the glory which shall be revealed in us!*" (Romans 8:18, KJV) Yes,

Father, even in the pain and suffering, glory is coming out of this! I thank you for an increase of Your glory! I thank you for a great gain of materialistic things as well. I thank you that I will live to see the goodness of the Lord in the land of the living!

I am grateful, Lord, that though pain is present, You haven't changed Your mind concerning me! You're still the same God that knows my beginning and my ending! You're the same God that knows the thoughts toward me; they're thoughts of peace, not of evil, to give me an expected end. Thank you that even through this pain, my expected end is great!

Healing

Yes, I believe, as the songwriter penned, "You are the Lord that healeth thee! You are the Lord, my healer! You sent Your Word to heal my disease. You are the Lord, my healer!" Lord, I ask You to heal me! I ask You first to heal my spirit man! I have become distracted during loss and lost my focus on You! I stopped praying and reading my Bible. I ask You to revive my spirit man! Holy Spirit, breathe on me again! Breath of God blow on my spirit man. I receive the healing and resurrection of my spirit man!

I recognize my inner man needs healing. I've been allowing all my emotions to govern all aspects of my life during this season instead of allowing You Lord to govern my world. I apologize. I decree and declare stabilization of my emotions! My emotions will not be all over the place. Even when there may be a roller coaster of emotions, my emotions will quickly become stable. I won't be sad always. I won't find myself in a constant state of depression. I give You my inner man! Heal! Heal!

Lord, heal my mind! I give You, my mind! I cast down imaginations and every high thing that exalts itself against the knowledge of God and bring into captivity every thought to the obedience of Christ. My mind is sound. I will have the mind of Christ. The enemy will no longer torment my mind! As You heal my mind, I make a conscious decision to do what Philippians 4:8 says and think on things that are true, honest, just, pure, lovely, and of a good report. Here's my mind, Lord! Lord, please forgive me for not thinking correctly! I embrace Your strength and help!

Lord, I thank you for healing my body! I decree and declare all body systems: digestive, endocrine, circulatory, respiratory, nervous, integumentary, reproductive, muscular, skeletal, lymphatic, urinary, immune, excretory, and musculoskeletal will function the way You designed them to function. All diseases trying to attack the body's systems are bound in Jesus' name! I embrace the restoration of health according to Your Word in *Jeremiah 30:17- "For I will restore health unto thee, and I will heal thee of thy wounds."* It's Your desire that I mayest prosper and be in good health, even as my soul prospers.

I speak to pneumonia, HIV/AIDS, cancer, all tumors, diabetes, hypertension, fibroids, thyroid problems, sickle cell anemia, asthma, bronchitis, sinusitis, arthritis, bursitis, scoliosis, appendicitis, pancreatitis, hernias, glaucoma, cataracts, back pain, schizophrenia, anxiety, depression, bipolar, PTSD, OCD, panic attacks, and post-partum depression. You must leave me, and my family's lives. The Blood of Jesus covers us! In the name of Jesus, I come against strokes and aneurysms. I arrest you before you try to come near my family or me.

My faith will not waver by what I see or feel. I believe You're able to heal because it's who You are. Yes, with men, it may look impossible, but with You, all things are possible. The report of my healing is already written.

I am receiving Your healing spirit, soul, and body. Thank you, Jehovah Rapha, the Lord who heals! I still believe there's a Balm in Gilead, and healing is mine!

<u>Provision</u>

Father, it's been a hard place related to loss. I've been used to my loved one being the provider of the family. I don't even know where to begin paying bills. You know my income has drastically changed. I don't know how I am going to make ends meet. I ask You, Lord, please be who You are and support me, provide for us I stand on Your Word *Psalm 37:25 (KJV)- "I've been young, and now am old; yet have I not seen the righteous forsaken, nor his seed begging bread."* I believe I am not going to have to beg for anything. I believe You're sending men to give unto my bosom. I can't see it now! I receive the financial blessings of the Lord, and decree money is coming to me and my house!

<u>Thank you!</u>

Lord, it may not make sense to anyone to say thank you to You in this moment! I thank you for the pain! I believe this pain is a divine setup to greatness. I thank you. I am able to see who You are in the midst of a place that I don't like. I thank you! It was You who kept my mind! I could've been in a mental institution unaware of my name with the amount of pressure I've endured and am enduring. I want to tell You thank you!

Lord, even when I wanted to end my own life! You kept me alive for such a time as this! I thank you for life! I thank you for sustaining me as I continue to live! Yes, I am going to continue to live and not die.

I thank you for being my head lifter. It's because of You that I can hold my head up in the midst of loss! I thank you for being a Good Father and always taking care of me. You, Lord, have been consistent in my world and even when I feel alone, You are there. Thank you, Father, for always being present and never leaving me or forsaking me.

Thank you, Lord, for loving me even when I was angry with You! You still loved me and cared for me the same! Thank you for Your love!

Thank you for grace and mercy! Thank you for not giving me what I deserved. Thank you that You didn't give me stale mercy but brand-new mercies every day. Thank you for daily loading me with benefits! I thank you, Lord! Yes, thank you for Your many benefits! Thank you, Jesus!

Please forgive me for murmuring and complaining. I apologize for always wanting more, even during loss, and not being thankful for what and who remains. Thank you for increasing what I have left! Lord, I want to thank you! I love and appreciate You!

Salvation

I don't want to assume everyone who is reading this book has accepted the Lord as your personal Savior. If you haven't accepted the Lord as Savior, I offer you Jesus, the best gift I can offer.

Accepting the Lord as Savior is as simple as repeating this prayer: I confess that I am a sinner and Jesus I want Your gift of Salvation. I believe Jesus Christ died on The Cross for my sins. I believe Jesus was buried and rose from the grave for me. I accept Jesus into my heart and believe that He saved me. Thank you, Jesus, for saving me!

Next, find a Bible believing and Bible teaching church. You're more than welcome to worship with my Pastors Joseph & Co-Pastor, LaQuisha Brown, at the House of Healing, DMV. You can find out additional information by visiting the website www.houseofhealingdmv.com

About the Author

Carol J. Williams called to the Kingdom for such a time as this. Carol is the founder of I Care Solutions, formed to educate and equip grieving individuals. I Care Solutions also improves the lives of the broken and disenfranchised. She's a Registered Nurse, Author, Speaker, Advanced Grief Recovery Method Specialist, Ordained Elder, and former radio talk show host.

She's had the opportunity to serve as Director of Education for the HIV/AIDS Awareness Program and Founder/President of Jewels Causing Change for Christ Women's Ministry.

The Lord has allowed Carol to share the message of hope globally. She believes her steps are ordered by the Lord and lives by the motto, "If I can help somebody as I pass along the way, then my living shall not be in vain."

Thank you!

Thank you, Lord, for allowing me to complete this book. I pray You're pleased, and it brings You glory in the Earth!

Thank you to my family! I love and appreciate you!

Thank you, Emily Claudette Freeman and Pecan Tree Publishing Company; I appreciate you!

Thank you, Pastor Joseph Brown, Co-Pastor LaQuisha Brown, and the House of Healing, DMV, for your prayers and support.

Thank you to all my friends who stayed in my world! I don't want to start calling names for fear of missing anyone. I love and appreciate each of you.

I am blessed to have several ladies who are influential in my life. You have inspired me in so varying ways. I wanted to acknowledge your impact on my life publicly. I appreciate you, Co-Pastor LaQuisha Brown, Larisha Warner, Sabria Mathis, & Theresa Royal Brown.

A special thanks to the members of Strength for the Grieving by the Grieving; I am thankful for you embracing the vision God has given me and your continued support and prayers.

Lastly, thank you to all the intercessors who consistently keep me covered!

And we say to these things, To God Be ALL the Glory!

Carol J. Williams

For speaking engagements or further information
Email: icaresolutionscw@gmail.com
website: www.icaresolutions.website